STORIES I CAN TELL

Feb. 2005

To ~

Harold & Clarice Turner

STORIES I CAN TELL

M.B. Elliston

M.B. Elliston

Copyright © 2004 by M.B. Elliston.

Library of Congress Number:		2004098289
ISBN:	Hardcover	1-4134-7420-9
	Softcover	1-4134-7419-5

All rights reserved. No part of this book may be reproduced or transmitted in any form or by any means, electronic or mechanical, including photocopying, recording, or by any information storage and retrieval system, without permission in writing from the copyright owner.

This book was printed in the United States of America.

To order additional copies of this book, contact:
Xlibris Corporation
1-888-795-4274
www.Xlibris.com
Orders@Xlibris.com
24247

CONTENTS

CHAPTER ONE: EARLIEST MEMORIES

    Goin' Fever 9

    Wind and Fire 11

    Down a Well 12

    Trouble in a Pig Pen 13

    A Kissing Lesson 14

    Dealing with a Bully 15

    My Debonair Dad 16

    "Still Paying for My Wife" 17

    A Happy Family 18

CHAPTER TWO: PRAIRIE LIFE

    The Great Depression Hits 20

    Getting By 21

    Burnt Wood, Bent Nails 23

    The Coffee Can Baker 24

    The Soap Salesman 25

Finding Fun 26

Tiny and Trixie 28

Plums and Rattlesnakes 30

Getting Around 32

A Road Trip 35

Church Folk 39

My Last Ride with Old Paint 40

The Rabbit Drives 42

A Rough Ride 42

101 Horns 43

CHAPTER THREE: GREEN THUMBS IN WEST TEXAS

Still Pioneers 46

Beating the Frost 48

Truck Farming 49

A Stetson for the Banker 52

The Potato Master 52

A Turnip Crop 55

The Biggest Harvest 56

CHAPTER FOUR: COLLEGE DAYS

Working the Mill 59

A Summer Selling Books 62

Ambulance Driving 65

"The Eyes of Texas" 66

Courting 66

The Diplomat's Car 68

Picturing Success 69

CHAPTER FIVE: CHURCH BUILDING

Where were you? 73

Free Furniture 74

The "Chapel of Faith" 76

Spreading the Word 79

Kernersville 82

Greenville and Wilmington 83

The "Lazy Preacher" 84

CHAPTER SIX: TAKING CARE OF BUSINESS

The Catalina Motel 86

The Carwash 88

The Shopping Center and Apartments 90

My Three Sons 91

CHAPTER SEVEN: (SORT OF) SETTLING DOWN

    Big Trips 95

    Back to Carolina 97

    Walnut Cove 99

    Selling the Farm 100

    My Dog Bear 101

    From One Pepper Seed 105

    Looking Back from Here............................... 106

CHAPTER ONE

Earliest Memories

Goin' Fever

I was born July 2, 1919, in Coleman, Texas, though I don't remember it. So I'll start out with what I did since age four, because that's the earliest I can recall.

When I was four, my Dad put me, my two sisters and my Maw into his Model T, and we went to Roby, Texas. In those days, the roads were dirt on good days, mud on bad days, and bogs on the worst days. The road had recently flooded, and on the way to Roby, we bounced through a bunch of gaping mud holes before one finally caught us. The front tire landed in a hole and the back tires were just spinning. We weren't going anywhere.

For some reason, getting stuck in the mud bothered me

terribly. Maw and Dad got out to gather some straw and wood to fill up the hole and get us going, and I stayed in the back of the truck and just bawled and bawled. You could have heard me for four country miles, I was crying so loud. That's the first thing I remember in my life, and Dad told me later that it was true, that every time we hit a mud hole I'd start bawling.

There's another reason the memory's so sharp. While I was pitching a fit in the truck, I watched my parents work on getting us out of the hole. All of sudden, there was Maw with a great big armload of brush, and we saw something moving on top of it. She saw it about the time I did: A great big snake was wriggling around in her sticks. She hollered and dropped her load, and the snake slithered away. Then Maw had something to cry about too.

When we got to Roby, we didn't have a place to live, so we made arrangements with a rancher to pitch a tent on his property. We lived there, in a tent on the prairie, for several months, for most of one summer.

One of my earliest memories there is playing in our campfire, poking sticks in it, and my dad warning me to quit doing it. Well, I kept on doing it anyway, and when I smacked a log to see the sparks shoot off of it, a little burning coal shot out and landed between my toes. You talk about hurtin'—I should have listened to my dad.

Well, we needed a house to live in, so one day Dad and I went to see some carpenters who were working on a house. He asked them if he could hire them, but they said they were backed up, had seven more houses to do, so they couldn't build one for us. However, they said, why don't you just watch what we're doing, and then you'll know how to build your own. And that's exactly what we did. Dad learned as he watched them, and then we bought a corner and built a house on it.

Then Dad decided to raise chickens, and eventually we had about 2,000 of them. One day, we looked out the window, and the chickens were all walking sideways at the edge of the yard, trying to get away from something. It was a big bull snake and it had been eating their eggs. Dad captured the snake, and as a joke, he tried to give it to Maw, who promptly locked the screen door and wouldn't come out of our house.

Before long, we sold the chickens and decided to move on. This would be no ordinary move, because Dad did something very unique: He built us a house on wheels, a house on a Model T truck. All five of us lived in it for about six months. I'll bet it was the first mobile home ever built in the United States. It was certainly the first one we'd ever seen in Texas in the 1920s. Naturally, this made quite an impression on me.

One spring day Dad took us for a drive in Deaf Smith County. As we neared the top of a large, rocky rise, we pulled over to have a look at the scene. I was five years old. I walked up the bank and found myself surrounded by flowers. As I picked a few of them, I surveyed the scene, and suddenly a kind of dream came over me—a yearning to travel. That's when the "goin' fever" got me, and it's had a hold of me ever since. From then on, I knew, I'd always have the urge to go, go, go.

Wind and Fire

Then we lived in a house on the prairie that faced south. Our windmill was in front of the house, and when the furious windstorms would come, it would whip around and around. Then when we had a dry spell, with no wind at all, we couldn't pump the water out of the ground, because the wells were 200 feet deep.

But what really fascinated us kids, what made our imaginations run wild, were the prairie fires. We'd go from window to window in the house watching the fires in all directions, because the county we lived in was mostly nothing but prairie grass, and the fires would spread all around.

It wasn't unusual to see several different fires at once, and it was really frightening. Since we were just little kids, we always worried that the fire would jump the lines and come our way. In fact, some of our neighbors kept a turning plow at the edge of their yard, and made sure they knew where the harness was, so that they could quickly plow a fire break around the garden when these great prairie fires came.

Down a Well

In one of our first houses growing up, we set up a gutter system that deposited all of the rain water in a cistern. We didn't have any city water, so for a time that was our sole water supply. We'd use it year round for drinking, cleaning ourselves, doing the wash, watering the animals, you name it.

We dug a hole for the cistern, about 20 feet deep to store extra water. Using a pulley, we'd lower a bucket into the cistern whenever water was running low. But one day, the rope on the bucket broke, so the bucket was floating on the water a dozen feet below the ground. How could we get it? Dad looked at his four-year-old son Melvin and had a flash: He'd lower me down to get it.

So he got a chain and tied it to a big bucket, and tied it up so that it couldn't turn over. Then I hopped in it, and he slowly lowered me down. No doubt, it was a dangerous operation, but our water was mighty important to us.

When I got down to the water level, I nabbed the old bucket and then he hoisted me back up, no problem. It was a startling experience, for sure. That's probably why it's one of the first things I remember.

A familiar scene from childhood: My Maw, a milk cow, my sisters, some chickens and me.

Trouble in a Pig Pen

When I was about five years old, we took a trip across town to see my Aunt Leora and her family. I had a cousin there, Chester, who was about my age, and that day we were fascinated by the family's pigs. Their old sow had recently given birth to 13 piglets, the cutest little things you ever laid eyes on.

They were running all around, and we decided we'd catch one so we could pet him. But every time we'd get close to one of them, they'd scurry off into a hole with their mom, the old sow. She was a big creature, over 500 pounds. Now, I'd never had any experience with pigs before, so I wasn't sure what to do and had to follow Chester's lead. That turned out to be a bit of a mistake, because he told me to chase a little pig away from the sow so he could catch it.

Well, I got in the pen with the sow, and she was busy eating. So I chased all the piglets out, and Chester caught one in his hands. The one he caught started squealing bloody murder. That got mama sow's attention. She turned around, opened that huge mouth of hers, and took after me in the pen! It was a small pen, about 14 feet square, so there wasn't a whole lot of room to move.

I may not have known much about pigs, but I was certain there wouldn't be a piece of me left if that sow got me. I ran like the dickens and got over the fence, with her mouth right behind my rump. We let her piglets back in, and that settled that. But I sure was shook up, and with the exception of a few county fairs, I made it a point to never get near another pig pen again.

A Kissing Lesson

When I turned six, my parents put me in public school for the first grade, in a one-room school house with about 25 students. And let me tell you, that's where I learned more about girls and sex and devilment in the first six months than I would learn for the rest of my life.

Our teacher was a big woman, and she liked to play volleyball. She played hard, and her socks would droop down to her ankles and her dress would always be flying up in the air—so us boys sat around and watched for her garters.

It was very educational, alright. Another time, I thought the girl sitting next to me was pretty, so I asked her if I could kiss her. Well, she went straight to the teacher, who didn't like the sound of that. The teacher called me up to the front of the class and blistered my hand with a ruler. You might say I learned an important lesson from that: I decided to never ask another girl—I'd just go ahead and kiss 'em.

Dealing with a Bully

One day, we were walking home from school, which was less than a mile away, but then our school bully stepped in the way. I was with a little buddy, Carl, who the bully abused all the time—at least when I wasn't around. On this afternoon, we decided we'd had enough of that. I said, "Carl, you go around and grab him by the legs from the back, and I'll take the punches in front, until we can get him down on the ground. And then we'll teach him a lesson he'll never forget."

The plan worked, and the big bully went down, but we had to scrap with him for awhile. Meanwhile, cars were stopping and people emptied out to watch the fight, and they were cheering for us little boys. We didn't need any encouragement, but we sure got it from the crowd.

That might have been the end of it, but before you knew it, I saw one of my sisters leading a teacher out to our house—he had come to see my Dad. The teacher explained that us boys had gotten into a fight, and asked what he should do about. Dad said, "Just do whatever the rules say to do."

Well, after that, I knew something was coming, so I started wearing three pairs of wool pants every day. I was going to be ready if there was to be any whoopings. And on the third day I wore triple-pants, sure enough, the teacher called us three boys into his office.

He started with Carl, and I was surprised to see how it went. The teacher gave him just three light licks with a leather belt. Then, he called me forward, and gave me the same light treatment. Especially with my layers of pants, I couldn't feel a thing. But when it came to the bully, the punishment was different. He'd broken lots of rules before, and the teacher gave him a thrashing. It gave him something to think about for several days afterward.

For Carl and I, it was a happy ending: After we teamed up on that bully, he never laid a finger on either one of us again.

My Debonair Dad

My parents, Custer Dee Elliston and Mary Sanders Elliston, were born and bred in Texas. They were first-generation Seventh-Day Adventists. They joined the church after they bought an SDA book from a colporteur. Then Dad hitchhiked to Amarillo to find some church men, and he invited them to our town to hold an effort to start a church there. My folks and their relatives formed a large part of that church as it got off the ground. My grandmother and several of her sons and daughters joined along with us.

The next year, Dad, who had been farming, decided to go sell books for the church. He'd go on sales trips in that house-on-a-truck we'd all stayed in. He'd drive it all around Texas selling the religious texts and Bibles, then stay in it at night.

Dad was one polished dude when he was selling those books house to house. He'd wear a suit, a hat, and starched, stiff white collars and cuffs. It wasn't the easiest place to sell books—people didn't always welcome salesmen to their door. But he made do, no matter the circumstances. One day, a pack of vicious dogs came out to meet him, but somehow they just hushed when they got near him. And then he went on and sold a book at that house.

My loving parents, Mary Sanders Elliston and "CUSTER dee elliston"—that's how he always wrote his name.

"Still Paying for My Wife"

It was funny how my parents came to know each other. Funny and costly.

Custer, the young man who would become my father, was living in Hereford, out on the prairie. One night, he went to a dance where he saw a cute red-headed girl, about 17 years old. She was dancing with a nice-looking fellow, but Custer didn't let that stop him. He walked up to the fellow, tapped him on the shoulder and said, "Next dance." That was the tradition then, and the man obliged.

And that's how Dad met Mary Sanders, the woman who would be my mother. He took her away from the other fellow—not knowing, of course, that that gentleman would later became the tax assessor for Lubbock County, where we would wind up one day.

Dad eventually bought several properties in the county, and every year that fellow would run up the taxes on Dad's lands. He ran them up and up and up until they reached $3,900. We all knew it was too high; the best land in Lubbock wasn't evaluated that highly, and Dad's land was in east Lubbock, which was the poor side of town.

So every year when he paid taxes my Dad would say, "I'm still paying for my wife."

Later, Dad gave the land to me. The first thing I did was contact the local tax assessors. I told them what had happened and asked them to reevaluate. "I'm taxed as though this property was ten times its size, and I need some relief," I said, pleading for a new review. "All I want is fairness."

Well, they did a new assessment and lowered the taxes to $680! I guess my Dad had been paying for his wife after all.

A Happy Family

We went through some austere times, early on, but things always seemed to work out for us. For a while, Maw worked as a midwife to a number of people, including a local judge. Luckily for us, the judge had a son who was about my age, but he was always growing like a weed, so every year I'd get about a dozen pieces of clothing from him. It was more clothes than I ever had use for. Kindnesses like that helped us get by when money was tight.

Through it all, we never even knew we were poor. That subject never came up at my house—even when we lived in a one-room, concrete-floor garage for seven years. We didn't have a bath inside the house until 1938! But again, we didn't worry too much about the conveniences of life, we just made out like it was. We had a rather simple life. And we were happy with it, a happy family.

CHAPTER TWO

Prairie Life

The Great Depression Hits

In the late 1920s, Dad was working as a plumber's helper in Hobbs, New Mexico, and making $3.50 an hour, which in those days was big money. But then, in just a day, everything changed. On October 29, 1929—"Black Tuesday"—the stock market crashed and the economy began to crumble. The Great Depression was upon us.

Dad didn't waste any time adapting to the new reality. As soon as he saw the news about the stock market in the morning papers, he went straight to the telegraph office and sent an urgent message to Maw. He told her to put ads in the paper that very day, offering just about everything we had for sale.

We had seven cars—cheap ones, just $20 Model Ts—and we sold six of those. We had 2,000 laying hens, which we sold for a dollar a piece. We had 13 head of registered Guernsey heifers that we were going to start a dairy with, and we sold all of them for $500 total. (The fellow who bought them couldn't afford to pay at the time, but for years afterward he made up for it by brining us huge shipments of corn, which we had plenty of need for.)

Maw also rented out our two rental houses and our own house for a year's lease. That's when we built a one-room concrete house with no indoor bathroom, and all of us—my folks, my two sisters and I—would live in it for seven years.

So within a few days, we had all of that done, before it really set in for the rest of the country that a major depression had hit. I don't know how Dad knew to do this, but he sure saved the day for us.

Getting By

Meanwhile, we kept on working, hard as ever. "When you get to the end of your rope," we would say, "just tie a knot in it and hold on." There were lots of big and small ways that we got by, living on the prairie during the depression.

During those years, there wasn't much growing, and often there wasn't much around for us to burn for fuel in the winter. And it could get awfully cold in that part of Texas in the winter, sometimes even dipping below zero degrees. So we got creative: We went out on the prairie where the cattle were kept and picked up what we called "surface coal." We'd fill up our gunny sacks and wagons with the stuff. And I'll tell you, nobody on the earth has ever made biscuits as good as the ones Grandma Elliston made using those cow chips to cook with.

For a while, Dad tried his hand as a trapper, to earn extra income. He ran trap lines daily for coyotes, skunks, badgers and swifts (a type of fox), and for a while we made a living off of him selling them for pelts.

We also raised poultry. We had a route selling both eggs and chickens for cooking. There was a market for that, because city folks didn't know how to keep a chicken, and we didn't have them in the supermarket like we do now. So it was a real good market.

When I got a little older, I decided, with Dad's permission, to buy three acres adjoining our family's land. It had better soil than the land our family lived on. I built a shed to put a nanny goat in, and to put my 36 Rhode Island Red hens in. I also had a cow that gave 4½ gallons of milk a day, so we'd always plant a few bushels of wheat for the cow to eat.

Well, I thought I had it made: I was only 12 years old, but I had a cow giving milk and chickens laying eggs, and a bicycle route where I'd go sell both. I charged 15 cents for a half a gallon, and delivered it to people's homes. I had great fun doing that before and after school.

One morning before school I went over to look after my chickens. I didn't see them, not in the chicken house, and there weren't any holes in the wire around it, so they couldn't have escaped. All I found was two sickly chickens that had been left by whoever took my hens during the night—someone stole them. Anyhow, I never did replace them, so I was out of the chicken business.

But I did start buying cows, ones they would bring into

the packing plant. Milk cows were selling for three dollars a piece, and if you kept them for awhile you could sell them for five or six dollars. I'd milk them too, and sell the milk until I sold the cow.

Then I decided, at age 13, to build three houses on my acreage and rent them out—all by myself. I had a little money that I'd put in the rat hole, from selling goat's milk, cow's milk, eggs and vegetables. So I built the three houses and rented them out for $3.50 a month. That gave me a start in life, and early on gave me a taste of the real estate business.

I had a good thing going, even for the depression days. Like I say, we didn't know we were poor. We just lived and enjoyed life.

Burnt Wood, Bent Nails

Shortly after that, when I was about 16, there was a big fire at a lumberyard in town, and some of the wood had just been scorched, so it was not a total loss. So Dad decided that it was time for us to build a six-room house. We arranged to get the burned and scorched lumber given to us for free—we just had to haul it off. We even pulled nails out of some of that wood, and then we'd straighten the nails and use them on our house. I mashed a lot of fingers doing it, but we got the house built. We found a fine carpenter who built the doors and windows for a dollar each.

We lived in that house for two years before we put a bath in it. I had a room of my own for the first time in my life. We stuccoed it on the outside and sheet-rocked it on the inside, and we had first-class living.

Building that house was a big reminder that in those days, you had to improvise. You had to be a self-made pioneer to get by.

The Coffee Can Baker

For a while, we also did seasonal work on a farm, both Dad and I. I was big and strong, for a youngster, and I proved it every day. They had 19 men working on the hay bailer, but not one of those strapping men could tail the bailer like I did. I lifted the bails and stacked them as fast as the mule would carry the bailer. I did it for 50 cents a day; Dad was paid a dollar a day.

We did this for a couple years, until one day in 1931 when we came in after the other hands had left, because we'd worked late. It was a Friday, time to get paid for the week's work. But this old hard-headed fellow, one of the bosses, wouldn't pay us yet. "You two help me milk all the cows, and then I'll pay you," he said.

Dad responded quickly. "We'll be sitting here on the porch until you finish milking, and then we'll pick up our paychecks," he said. That was the last day we ever worked anywhere, for anybody, for wages. We decided it was time to step out and step up.

That was a big day for us, because Dad had a lot of ideas, and now we could get around to pursuing them.

He started by developing a new gas oven to bake in, and came up with his own unique brand of whole wheat bread. Here's how he did it: He went to the scrap heap and found two coffee cans to bake the bread with. He'd connect the two cans together, and bake the dough inside them. When the loaves came out, they were a foot long, and round.

Dad began to sell it for 10 cents a loaf, which was twice the normal price of bread at the bakeries in town. But before long, his bread was selling out.

The big bakeries didn't like the competition. They'd stack their bread on top of his at the stores so that it would mash up the round loaves. Dad said, "Well, I'll whip that too." So he went and built hundreds of glass dispensers especially for his bread.

People were so crazy about that bread that we couldn't keep up with the demand. We ran that home bakery for several years. I think Dad never should have gotten out of it. His recipe was so good, he should have been Pepperidge Farm.

The Soap Salesman

One day we were out in the front yard cleaning up some potatoes and putting them in bushel baskets to take to market, and this traveling salesman came by toting a leather bag. Without introducing himself or anything, he just assumed my Dad was looking for a bargain.

"I'm selling soap," he said. He sat his bag down on the ground and reached in, pulling out a couple bars. "This is a very special bar, and it sells in the store for a dollar. But I'll give it to you half-price: two for a dollar."

Dad just looked at him. So the man reached back in his bag and got another one and said, "I'll throw this one in too, for just a dollar." Dad just stared. And so the salesman kept reaching in the bag and adding bars, saying after each one that we could have them all for a dollar. Before long, he had those bars of soap stacked up the full length of his arm, all the way to his chin!

"I'll still let you have *all this soap* for just one dollar," he said, again.

Finally my Dad spoke. "That's too much d__n soap for a fellow who only takes one bath a year," he said.

Needless to say, the salesman dropped that arm-full of soap in the bag and left in a hurry.

Me and my two sisters, Margaret and Mildred, at one of our family farms.

Finding Fun

You might ask, out there on the prairie back then, what did children do for fun? Well, it was up to us—we had to figure out something to do. And we figured it out alright.

One thing we liked to do involved a stick of bubblegum, all chewed up and attached to a string. We'd dangle and push this wad of gum around the little holes in the dirt that we could find all over the place. These weren't just any holes: They were tarantula nests. The tarantulas, you see, would get all riled up by the intrusion, our gum there, and lash out at it, attack it. And when they did, they'd stick right to it.

We'd pull them out, put them in a jar, and carry them around. We'd take the big ones to school and show them to our teacher. We had real fun tarantula hunting, real fun. We'd do it by the hour and sometimes by the day.

Then there were some bigger holes we paid attention to: prairie dog holes. The prairie dogs were harder to get acquainted with, however. Whenever we'd come around, one of them would start barking at us and telling all the others to get back in their holes. You might say we never got much from the prairie dogs, but it was fun stalking them.

You'd be surprised at some of our other experiences with creatures. One day, late in the summer, Dad was irrigating a field, and the water eventually got too high for a nearby den of skunks. A mama skunk and four of her babies came out. Dad caught them and brought them home in a sack. I asked him what he was going to do with them. "We're going to operate on them," he said. "We're going to take their stink bags out and keep them as pets."

Well, this should be rather interesting, I thought. Dad took the creatures out to the shed, and got out the tools he used to operate on chickens. He removed their stink glands and sewed them back up, and they healed up fine.

Then, believe it or not, they did indeed become our pets. Us three kids named each of the skunks, got collars for them, and started leading them around on leashes. We took them everywhere, and kept them in a box in the house, because they were "clean" skunks from then on. They were just like kittens, and we sure enjoyed them, and in fact they made better pets than any cat you ever saw. They were also very helpful to us in our granary, where they did a super job of cleaning up all the mice.

One Saturday night, me and my sisters, Mildred and Margaret, decided to take them to town. We went down near the department stores, and every time we'd pass a person on the street, the skunks would stick their tales in the air! Some folks were alarmed, but the police, they just liked the entertainment. We did that all summer, having fun with the skunks wherever we went—everywhere but church that is.

When it came to cooking up some fun, my neighbor, Raymond Puckett, and I spent some great times together. In the early 1930s, when we had a free day, we'd go hunting. There was a giant ranch nearby, some 37,000 acres, and we'd drive into it and go hunting all day.

We were after cottontail rabbits. Of course, when we got near them, they'd run because of our noise, and scamper into their holes. Still, they'd peek out at us, and that's when we'd shoot them. We'd get anywhere from 6 to 16 rabbits a day. We'd skin them, dress them, and then go sell them as meat for 15 cents a piece. We made some spending money that way.

And we spent it together. We'd go pick up the school teacher's two daughters, you see, because Raymond was interested in one and I was interested in the other. Then we'd stop by the drug store and buy two quarts of ice cream. Our next stop was the state park, where we would park. A couple of us would sit on the back, and a couple in the front, and we'd each share a quart of ice cream with our dates. That was an evening of entertainment for us—all paid for with the money we'd made from the rabbits.

Tiny and Trixie

In 1934, we lived on the highway east of Lubbock. We had a little half-breed Boston Screwtail dog that was female, and a friend of ours had a nice registered dog that was male. We bred them and came up with seven pups, two of which we kept.

Tiny was a little thing, and built real low to the ground. Trixie, on the other hand, was long and lanky and stood up tall. Two days after they were born, sadly, their mother got run over by a car and killed.

So we figured we'd have to raise them ourselves. At first we started bottle feeding them, but then it turned out that we had some unexpected help. About that time, a mother cat who had evidently lost some kittens recently came to live with us. Well, if you can believe it, Dad put that cat in the little bed we'd made for the dogs, and she adopted them! She even nursed them, as though they were hers from the beginning. It was a most unusual thing.

One Saturday morning, when the pups were seven weeks old, Trixie let out a bark—her first one. With that, she discovered she was a dog instead of a cat, and she was so happy she barked all day.

Those dogs were wonderful pets, and we loved having them around and kept them for several years. They were quite different from each other. Tiny was my dog, according to both her choice and mine. One weekend, we all hopped in the pickup and headed north to visit a canyon near Amarillo. As we were driving along a road that paralleled a railroad, we came alongside a big, long freight train. About the time we were even with it, the train whistle let out a blast. And then my little Tiny, who had been sleeping on my lap, leapt up against the window and started barking and growling at the train. I'm sure she was saying, "Let me to it, I'll stop it from waking *me* up!" And she kept making a fuss until that train was out of sight.

Another time, there was a big sow that got out of the packing plant and walked over toward our place. And I do mean big, perhaps 600 pounds. Well, Tiny didn't like the idea of that big hog hanging out near our fence, so she took out after the sow. She got a hold of its left ear, and held her grip a half a mile up and a half a mile back, with the sow running the whole way. What a commotion it was! The sow was squealing like it was the end of the world, and she was shaking her head the whole time she ran, with Tiny hanging on the whole time. I was afraid that Tiny would snip that ear right off and go flying into the sow's big mouth.

Finally, I caught up with them and snatched Tiny off of the sow. That nine-pound dog sure was bold, looking out for our interests like that. And she had survived some real danger.

Plums and Rattlesnakes

I was 12 years old when our neighbor, H.P. Glass, bought a new truck. He came over to see us one day and said, "Let's go plum hunting." Now, you sure couldn't find any plum trees where we were in West Texas, so a few of use joined him for a trip to the Brazos River.

We made our way there, to a spot near the river. Since we were going to be there for a few days picking plums, we made a nice bed in tall grass. Getting water was a little trickier than you might think, because the Brazos, where we were visiting it, had just about dried up. The river bed was half a mile wide, but during the daytime, no water flowed there. At night, there would be a little trickle that would run down the middle, but then the sun would rise and dry it up again. So to make sure we had some fresh water, we'd dig a hole right in the middle of that nighttime stream, and by morning we'd have a good little reservoir.

Well, we found a grove of plum trees, but they were pretty dry and the fruit was small. We went looking for bigger, better plums, and saw, in the distance, what looked to be a branch of the river with good, green trees growing on it. So we headed out for that spot, ready to pick plums by the bushel.

We had to walk though some tall grass to get there. I was in the lead of our group, and everywhere around me, on almost every sprig of grass, there were locusts. They were making plenty of noise: *ZZZZ, ZZZZ, ZZZZ, ZZZZ.*

All that buzzing worried the socks off of me, but then something worried me even more. I looked to my side, and there was a great big old ant hill; the ants were done with it, but right in the middle was a giant rattlesnake.

Well I tore out of there! But my Dad decided that we were going to get that snake. He grabbed a hold of its tail, and pinned its head to the ground with a stick. That was a tricky operation, because the snake kept coiling around dad's forearm, just squeezing away. Someone brought a gunny sack, and they were just about to drop it in when we heard another rattler—the snake had a partner nearby! And it sounded just like the locusts, the way it was buzzin': *ZZZZ, ZZZZ, ZZZZ, ZZZZ.*

Well, we nabbed that one too, and put it in another sack. Then it was my turn to get involved. Dad tied the gunny sacks to two ends of a long stick, and then he told me: "Melvin, you carry this back to the campsite, please." I was obedient, so I did what he told me to do—but you should have seen how scared I was, how carefully I walked with those snakes.

That same day, I picked a five-gallon jar full of nice plums. But after that run-in with the snakes, we were too scared to sleep in that tall grass, so Dad said, "Let's go sleep by the stream." As we slept, Dad had a dream about handling those snakes, and dreamed that one of them got out of his hand while he was capturing it. As he dreamed that, his body jerked around some and his hand went in the cold stream running next to him.

It scared the devil out of him! So the Good Lord got even with Dad for making me carry those rattlesnakes. And I brought home enough plums for a winter-long supply of good jam.

Getting Around

In the early 1920s, we witnessed what we considered to be one of the real phenomena of our time: an electric rail line that did runs over several parts of Texas. It was ahead of its time, this rail system and the facilities to run it. It had automatic stops at either end. After it was loaded up with cargo, the people who ran it would punch a button and it would go all the way to the end of the line, by itself, without a captain or anyone driving it.

We'd go down the depot in Roby and pick up our mail, which had just come in on the rail line from a town called Roatan. After we unloaded on our end, they'd punch a button and it would return to the other end of the line, again pilot-less. It was rather unusual, those days or any other days, and it was a huge help for us to have this rail line running.

But what really grabbed my attention was cars. We witnessed the first age of the automobile. Growing up in my generation, when cars came on the market, it gave everyone a tremendous appetite for obtaining and driving cars. For most of the 1920s, people were snatching up cars. But then, the Depression hit, and suddenly many folks had cars that they could no longer afford to put gasoline in. Consequently, that's when I began my own version of horse-trading: car-trading.

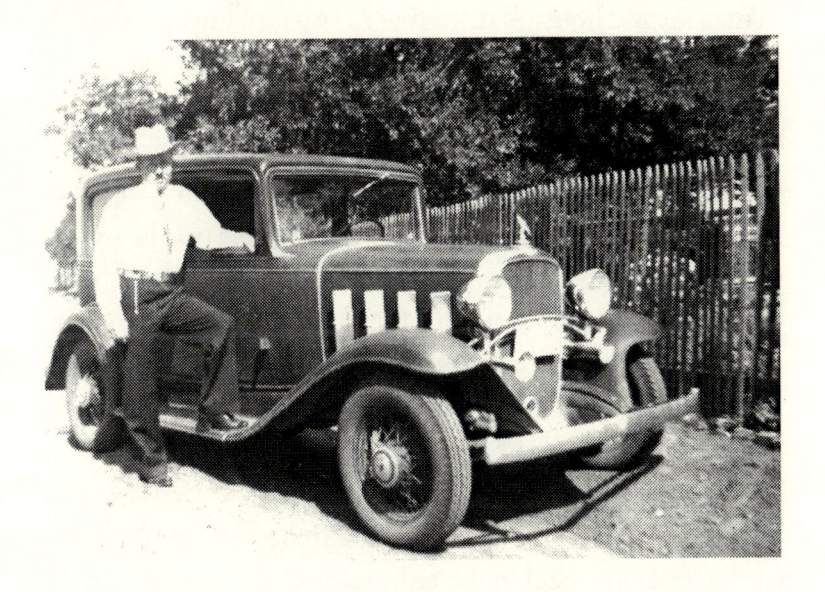

I started car-trading when I was just 14. Here's one of my first and favorite vehicles, a 1932 Chevrolet.

I went through one car after another, and began even before I was able to drive. I was 14, and a local man and his family were fixing to hitchhike back to their old home in East Texas, because they were broke. He said I could have his 1928 Model A Ford for $15.50, and Dad said I could buy it, so long as I didn't drive it.

Then, another fellow came by one day shortly thereafter when I was out in the field washing potatoes. He stopped and asked me if I'd be interested in a 1929 Model A Ford, with new tires on it. He wanted $15 for it. I said I wasn't sure, but I'd give it some thought. Again, I checked with

Dad, and he said I could buy it but not drive it. So I did, and it made for a great trading vehicle.

And then, a man came by with an interesting offer. He had a small lot and house in town that he was looking to get rid of, and he needed a car. He wanted to know if I'd be interested in a trade. It sounded good to me, but again I ran it by Dad, who had a quick answer. "This man wants to trade a house and lot for a $15 car? If he's got the deed, yeah! Trade with him!"

We drove over to look at the house, a simple two-bedroom in the poor part of town. There wasn't a stick of furniture in the place—the fellow and his family had slept on the floor. But I made the trade, and it turned out to be a super deal for a young man. I wound up selling the property for $150. For me, for anybody at the time, that was big money.

The next car I traded up to was a 1931 Model A. Later, I bought a 1932 Chevrolet, with a spare tire on the front fender and chrome flaps on either side of the motor. I drove it for two years and sold it at a good price.

Then, a man I sold milk to told me that his 1934 Chevrolet had burned up. It didn't look too good, but I thought it was still salvageable. The motor seemed OK—the fire didn't even melt the rubber off of the spark plugs. I told him I wanted to buy it, and he gave it to me for $50. Then I got to fixing it up. At the wrecking yard, I found a 1934 Pontiac sedan with a body that would fit on the Chevy. The body was brand new, without a scratch, and I bought it for $50. The body fit the frame almost perfectly. I drove that hybrid car for a little while then sold it for $450.

About that time, I decided to go off to high school at an academy down near Ft. Worth. I used that money from the Chevy/Pontiac sale to pay for the first year of tuition and board.

The only time I ever saddled up on a buffalo.

A Road Trip

In the early 1930s, me and a buddy, Doug Crump, got our heads together and decided to take a road trip. I had $43 and he had $46, so we set out on our journey with that money and a few things in a shoulder bag.

We started by hitchhiking, sticking our thumbs out at every car that came by. But not a one of them stopped. So we spread our blankets between the highway and train tracks, which turned out to be a bad idea, because the noise of the passing trucks and trains woke us up every ten minutes.

We got up about 4:00 a.m., dried off the dew that had settled on us, and set out thumbing again. Still, nobody would stop for us, so we walked 16 miles to the next town. There, we stopped for a little refreshment at a service station, where we noticed that there was a stripped-down Model T, a 1925 model, for sale. We kicked the tires and considered it a bit, like two 14-year-old boys could do, and ultimately decided to buy the vehicle. It cost us $40—$20 a piece. Gas was just 14 cents a gallon, so we could go a long way, we figured.

It was a really basic model, to say the least. It had no seat belts, and just a board for a seat. But we threw our bags in the back and set on down the road. Since we had transportation, we thought we could to a little truck gardening along the way. We bought one bushel each of squash, cucumbers and tomatoes. We started stopping at every little store along the way, but not a one of them would buy our vegetables. But we found a use for them: Driving down the road, we'd throw them at cows, pigs and goats until we ran out.

We drove that Model T a bit faster than it was supposed to be driven, and by the time we got to Waco, the rods in the engine started clicking a bit. So we found another service station and asked them if we could use their facilities to make some repairs. They said sure, and we got it all fixed up. From then on we drove a little slower, because we sure didn't want to throw a rod.

Our next destination was Houston, and we were anxious to get there, so we drove all day for two days. There, we decided to sell the Model T, which was starting to wear down. We found someone who took it off our hands for $20.

From there, we hitchhiked down to the nearby town of Alvin, where Doug had some relatives. We had a good night visiting them, and then Doug and his cousins decided to spend some time together, so I decided that I better go try to find some work. I walked down to a nearby dairy and hired on there.

They had a simple room for me, but it was hot as blazes in there. I'd sweat through the night and get up early in the morning to help milk the cows—real early. The hour of 2:00 a.m. may seem too early for a young fellow to get up and go to work, but that's what I did. I'd work three or four hours in the morning, and four or five in the afternoon. And I did it all week long. I wound up working for them for 30 days, at one dollar per day, so they were definitely getting their full value out of me.

One day, Doug and his cousins asked me to go to Galveston with them for some recreation. On the way, we saw a nice park where folks were swimming in the branch of a river, so we stopped and swam for the whole day. I got a terrible case of sunburn, but had a good time, because they gave me my first swimming lessons.

When we got to Galveston, I bought a big orange and bag of peanuts. Then they took me on my first roller coaster—and man, was it a big one. Let me tell you, a bellyful of food did not go very well with the ups and downs of a roller coaster.

When we got back home, I had some serious sunburn blisters on my shoulders. They got so bad I had to cover them with medicated cotton under my shirt. That put some serious thoughts in this boy's mind. After one more morning of milking cows, I decided it was time to go. That day I asked for my pay so I could be on my way. The boss man, though, didn't like the idea. "Son," he said, looking me straight in the eye, "you haven't even worked enough to pay your room and board, so you ain't getting nothing yet."

I decided it was time to check out. Doug was tied up with his cousins, whose family had just discovered oil on their property and were striking it rich. So I struck out on my own.

I was on my way in less than 30 minutes, thumbing my way again. I went all over the place, but the more I thumbed, the more my thumb pointed toward Lubbock, toward home.

On the way to the town of Junction, I caught a ride with a fellow who was delivering movie reels. He let me sleep in his truck at night, and the next morning he brought me out a couple of cups of coffee before he went off in another direction.

I started thumbing again, and a fellow in a brand new 1934 Chevy picked me up. Now, that coffee I had that morning was the first I'd ever had in my life, and my stomach certainly wondered what it was. And I didn't know that the Good Lord had built roller coasters around the town of Junction. We sped up and down those steep hills, and around sharp corners, one after another, and let me tell you, that coffee didn't sit well.

The fellow stopped at the next town, so there I found a young guy, about 21 years old, who had a Model A Ford roadster. I asked him if he could take me to the next town, and he said sure. He took off driving like crazy, and about the third turn out of town, there were two beautiful redheads by the side of the road, thumbing a ride. The driver looked at me and said, "Buddy, here's where you get out."

But I wanted to keep on going, so I asked him, "Can I ride on the running board, and hold onto the radiator cap?" He said, "Sure, if you've got the nerve." I held on tight as he roared on down the road. We must have hit 80 miles an hour, but I never let go.

My adventure came to an end a few days later, when I got into Lubbock about 3:00 in the morning. Dad came to the door in his union suit, welcomed me in and went to bed. I'd been gone five action-packed weeks, and I decided I'd never go on a safari like that again.

I put my hand in my pocket and pulled out my remaining money: I had a whopping 93 cents.

Church Folk

When we first arrived in Lubbock, the population was just 22,000. So we watched the city grow up to where it is today, with a population of almost 250,000.

We joined a church our first days there, a little church that we went to for years, until they sold it and got another one across town. (Dad donated all of the blocks for that new, big church and for the educational facilities next to it.) Church was important to us, and there our family made some of its closest friends.

To illustrate how much the friendliness of a church community meant to us, I'll mention this: Often times, a whole family would be invited to visit with another for the weekend, to celebrate our day of rest. On one particular weekend, for example, when I was a teenager, we invited a family of four to our place. We enjoyed a great lunch and dinner together, with coconut cake for desert. Then, us kids went out in the yard to play.

Again, this was a very close-knit community—sometimes a little too close. While we were playing, another set of family friends joined us. Normally that would have been just fine, but in this case there was a complication. This fellow, you see, was dating a school teacher who had once been engaged to one of the fellows who was already visiting with us. Well, things got hot in a hurry—these two gentlemen got agitated and headed straight for each other, and they met when their fists connected with their heads.

Both of them fell straight back, hitting the ground hard. It might have ended there, but then their families got into it. I can remember one of the gals stomping one of the men with her high heels!

Things finally quieted down, after a "good little church fight," as I called it. We finished out the weekend in good shape, as good of friends as we ever were. And I had been reminded that when a fellow grows up in a rural church, he's going to see all sorts of things happen.

My Last Ride with Old Paint

In the darkest days of the Great Depression, there eventually came a time when there was no feed left to sustain our animals. It was like that for everyone we knew. We'd sold most of our animals in 1929, when the economy crashed, but kept a few to help us out. We sold our milk cows, but we did have a nanny goat that gave three quarts of milk a day—now that's a lot of milk from a goat. And in the early 1930s, I had a horse, a gelding, named Old Paint. I think I paid about two dollars for him. He was white and brown, a beautiful horse.

I had Old Paint for about three years. He carried me to work at different farms, and brought me home, and spent a lot of time with me when I was home. He was good to me, he'd let my father and mother ride him. He loved us, and I was very fond of him.

It wasn't unusual for him to be standing right against the

fence where I was working, because he wanted to be there and I wanted him there. And every time I left to go plow a field, go to school or see a neighbor, he would nay and nay and nay. As I left, I could always hear him three or four miles down the road. We were almost as close as my dog Bear is to me now.

But the hard fact was that we had run out of food. President Roosevelt ran out of food, the states ran out of food—no one could afford to feed their cattle. That was before we started irrigating, and it was really dry. The ground got hard as a brick, and we simply couldn't raise enough grass for grazing.

Still, I tried my best to feed Old Paint. I cut young tumbleweeds, before they got stickers on them and still had some food value, and filled a shed with those before the winters so I could feed him when the cold came. Now and then I'd get a few heads of grain from someone and mix that in, so he'd have some vitamins in his diet, and I let him graze around the edges of what little grass there was.

But these were rough times, with absolutely nothing for animals to graze on for hundreds of miles around. In fact, my uncle would drive to New Mexico to get truckload after truckload of grain, just to keep his animals alive.

One fall, when things hit rock bottom, the government bought up the livestock on the ranges and destroyed them, so they wouldn't have to starve to death. That was when I took Old Paint for my last, long ride.

It was about three-and-a-half miles to the corrals, but it should have been a hundred miles farther than what it was. I let him walk the whole way, because I wanted to say my goodbye to him. When we got there, I pulled the bridal off of him, he rubbed his head on my shoulder, and then I closed the gate.

It had been a heavenly deal to have that horse. But there wasn't anything to do but cooperate with the government's program or let him starve to death, and of course I didn't want that to happen.

It's hard to tell you, but I'm going to tell you, that I cried all of the three-and-a-half miles on the walk back, with him neighing, "Don't leave me, stay with me," and "Hurry back" and everything else. But that was my last ride with Old Paint. And so, I said, "Goodbye Old Paint, I'll see you in the sky."

The Rabbit Drives

For a time, jackrabbits were so rampant that we considered them a plague. They would just ravage the grasslands, leaving nothing for the livestock to eat. So the state decided to put a bounty on them: five cents a piece, payable to anyone who brought in a pair of jackrabbit ears.

This led to an amazing spectacle. They called it a "rabbit drive." I went with Dad to observe some of these huge hunts. A large group of men, each of them armed with a shotgun, would spread out in a giant circle, then they'd all advance, doing their best to make sure no rabbit escaped the circle. Hunting this way, they'd get hundreds of pairs of ears for that bounty.

A Rough Ride

When I was a teenager, my Uncle Raymond and his three daughters, all of them cowgirls, invited me to help with a cattle drive. When we got to the roundup site, they had a horse by the name of Rocky for me to ride. Now, I was not a trained cattle driver, like my cousins were. After all, I was mainly a truck gardener at that point.

I was assigned a position to one side of the herd. For a while, I was riding along joyfully and enjoying it. But then, one maverick heifer decided to bolt. And of all the places for her to run, she chose my direction. Of course, my horse was well-trained for this, but his rider was not. Without any instruction from me, Rocky tore after the runaway.

Then, before I knew it, he stopped on a dime and gave five cents change, turning suddenly and sharply to the left. Unfortunately, I didn't follow suit.

Instead, I went flying over the saddle horn and into the dirt. You talk about hurtin'! Let's just say that that saddle horn caught me in the worst possible place.

Rocky was so well trained that he went on after the heifer and left me lying on the ground, where I moaned and groaned for half an hour. He brought the runaway in all by himself.

For me, it was a humbling experience, to take a fall in front of my cowgirl cousins.

101 Horns

I had an uncle, Berle Elliston, who rode the historic cattle drives along the Chisholm Trail. He did it for seven years, and we were always proud that he'd made it though all those rough rides alive.

Ours was a cattle culture, in many ways, and you could find ample proof of that in one of our somewhat unique family hobbies. Over the years, we amassed a sizable collection of mounted steer horns, in quite a range of shapes and sizes. We specialized in the longhorns.

My Dad built a huge collection of mounted longhorns. We've kept dozens of pairs as family heirlooms.

I made my first pair in 1934, when I was just a young 'un. When things were so dry, and the sand took over the grass, cattle were dying by the hundreds of thousands. There was simply no way to feed them all, so the government set up an emergency program to buy and exterminate thousands of cattle. They'd pay between three and seven dollars per head, just to get rid of all these starving cattle. So during one of those programs, I sawed the horns off of a steer and mounted them to put on the wall. I still have that set of horns today, 70 years later.

In years to follow, Dad made mounting, collecting and selling longhorns one of his many specialties. By the time he was done, I'll bet he handled more than 10,000 pairs. It was real fun to go with him when he'd go sell them. One summer in the early 1940s, we took a trailer load of horn sets to Rapid City, South Dakota, and Dodge City, Kansas to make some sales. Dad and I went looking for a place to sell a particularly big set, one that was seven feet across. I was surprised when he sent me into a veterans' club where they were about to have a floor show. There, the manager was really impressed with the horns, and said he'd pay me for two sets of them, if I'd just wait around until after the show. Well, what could I do? I had to make that sale, so I stayed.

Dad kept 101 choice sets of horns for himself, and today many trophies from that collection are hanging in my home and in the homes of many of my relatives. Some of them are so big that people don't believe they're real, but I can testify to the fact that they are.

Dad made some extra money hustling those horns, and he sure loved the hobby. For him, it was great recreation. Overall, the horns have been a wonderful relic and heirloom for the whole family. They've kept a bit of the old times with us, wherever we go.

CHAPTER THREE

Green Thumbs in West Texas

Still Pioneers

Having been born in Texas from ancestors who had long lived there, many things brought home the realization that these were still very much pioneer days and that we were still pioneers. Time and time again, we found that we had to work things out for ourselves, because we were going down trails that no one had gone down before.

So when we found ourselves in Lubbock during the days of the Great Depression, we realized that it was a survival of the fittest situation, and that we would have to get creative in order to get by. To make provision for your family was the main thing, and to try to keep your roots where you were, if possible. Of course, families by the droves had to move on, but we decided to stay where we were.

We could do so because, fortunately, Dad was a great pioneer. No matter how bleak things became, he could always think the thing through, see the whole picture, and devise a way for us to succeed.

Dad was reared on a farm where they mostly grew grains and corn. Maybe that's why he had a knack for watching the weather and predicting the patterns of the seasons. One day in 1923, he went outside, looked up at the sky and said, "We're going to have a real dry year. So I'm going to change-up my farming methods." This time, he didn't plow up the land before planting. Instead, he bought a bunch of seed, waited until there was one good rain, and just turned up a little sifting of dirt and planted the seed.

Lo and behold, after that shower, immediately the plants sprang up. When they hit about six inches, another nice shower came along. Since the plants were buried so shallow, the rain went right to the roots. So our plants grew better than everyone else's, because they'd buried their seed so deep the water wasn't getting where it needed to go.

I can remember my Grandpa saying, "The rest of us didn't even put a plow in the ground, but Custer just scratched around and raised the only maize in the county."

Our farming operations started simple: Dad built a one-room house that was about as wide as two garages, and we three kids and Maw and Dad lived in that house for seven years. We raised food in the garden: lettuce, carrots, spinach, onions and so on.

One morning, Mom and I went to town to try to sell some of the extras. But for all the grocery stores we visited, they only bought a total of 15 cents worth of vegetables. Dad said, "Well, we'll whip this thing." Then he went down to J.C. Penney and bought three red kid's wagons, and put each of us children on one going door to door with a wagon full of vegetables. People loved that, and we started to sell out. From there, our operation got bigger and bigger, and we did it for years.

Beating the Frost

Over time, from about 1930 onward, we moved into wholesale truck farming. Getting there wasn't easy. Dad really had to improvise to keep us competitive with the growers in the valley of South Texas. You see, their growing season put them as much as six weeks ahead of us, so growers in our area were always playing catch-up with them.

One way Dad got ahead was to start growing plants in early spring, while most of our neighbors were still waiting on the warm weather. Except for the cabbage and the collards, which we grew plenty of, most of the plants we grew would be killed off by any hard frost. So to keep the young plants going through the frost, with my help he built some highly useful cold frames.

Here's how we did it: We'd box up a small plot of land with boards, about 4 feet wide and 24 feet long, and place wire mesh over those boxes after we planted seed. Then, we'd get a bunch of thin cloth, "domestic cloth" we called it at the time, and coat it with paraffin, which would help keep the heat in. Then, we'd lay that cloth across the boxes, and cover it with another layer of the wire, to keep the cloth in place no matter how high the winds got.

The sun would warm those boxes during the day, and they held enough heat at night to keep the plants germinating, even while it was frosting. We did this for about three years, and the system worked great, but we outgrew it. Eventually, we were growing so many plants that we had to build our own greenhouse. Now, this wasn't a traditional greenhouse, as it wasn't made of glass. Instead, it was much like our cold frames, only much larger. We stretched waxed cloth over a huge wood-frame structure, and then we could germinate more plants than ever.

I was a farmhand from an early age.

Truck Farming

Another of Dad's schemes helped us a lot. We started growing plants in grape boxes, which were about the size of a big shoe box. That way, our plants were always fresh when we sold them—in fact, they were still growing. Using those boxes, we grew tomatoes, cabbage, onions, flowers, and all sorts of other plants. This put us ahead of other growers, because a plant pulled out of the soil is only going to keep so long, even if you keep it moist. But with ours, they'd keep for weeks; all the customers had to do was pour a little water in the box and then harvest the plants they wanted to eat.

That was a very profitable thing that Dad figured out. We began to truck farm in 1931, and because of his ingenuity, foresight and faith, we sold those boxes all over the West Texas plains. Over time, we got into mass production with this, to where we could beat out our competitors at the stores. We had several routes where we would deliver these plants we'd grown in the boxes.

That's really where I got my education, traveling all over the plains with my mother selling these plants. My parents made a beautiful pair. Dad was great at figuring out the growing, and Maw did all the sales work. She was a terrific salesperson. When she'd go into a store, and all the other truck gardeners would be there, the store buyers would listen to my mother ahead of all the men. And she always made the sale. She did that for us all the way until 1944.

It was amazing how well we were welcomed in little towns; and then we'd have calls to come on back and bring more plants. On our routes, which we'd make in a Ford van, we'd sell the plants to little grocery stores, hardware stores and service stations. We sold millions of plants, both at home and out on the road, and it worked out fine for us. God blessed our humble efforts the whole way.

One of our main routes, to give an example, was this:

We would leave Lubbock and go straight north, up through Abernathy, Hale Center, and then to Plainview. At Plainview, we turned west and went to the little towns out that way, like Shallow Water, Littlefield, etc. And then as we got on out as far as we would go, we'd come to a town called Muleshoe.

That was quite a frontier town, so to speak. Just beyond it, there was little but sand, and you could always see the sand moving about, even with a small wind. So much did it move around that it was a popular hunting ground for arrowheads. The sand would blow out and leave them lying right on top. Now and then you might see a sprig of grass, but not much more than that. It was quite an education to leave Lubbock on the plains, where there always some green, and to go to a place where there was none. We'd make that route about once a week.

There was a town by the name of Post on one of our other routes. We sold a few plants there, but we were really interested in this watermelon patch that we had heard about, located about 20 miles east of town. When we got there, we found that the patch was a peculiar thing of nature. The grower had fruit trees down in this deep sand which sat in this acreage below the surrounding terrain. And man, talk about growing fruit! Just out of that, in some sandy dirt he had planted a big watermelon patch, probably 30 to 40 acres worth. And they were giants! The watermelons were so big that you couldn't put too many in a pickup before the truck was almost sitting down on its tires. They were from 26 to 32 inches tall, and as for the eating, they were as fine as they come.

We bought them for five cents each, and we had to load them ourselves. Then we took them back to Lubbock, where we sold them for 25 cents each. We'd knock on doors when we'd get back home, and sell the load in 30 minutes. Dad said, "That's kind of profiteering off of people, to sell it for five times what you gave for it." He'd say that quite often, but we did that day after day after day. We had to work out these deals so that we could exist in those times.

A Stetson for the Banker

We did pretty well in the truck farming business, and got better at it over time. Every year Dad would ramp it up a bit. Our first year, which was 1930, he borrowed $50 from the bank to invest in the crops. The second year he borrowed $150, the third he borrowed $500, and the fourth he borrowed $1000. It got to the point where, one day when I went to town with my Dad, the banker said to him, "Well, are you ready to buy the whole bank?"

Everyone needed some backing if they were going to do business in the 1930s, so Dad cultivated a good relationship with the bank, and he had quite a ritual that went with all this. Each time Dad would go in to get a loan, he'd wear his overalls, work shoes and work hat. But when he'd go back in the fall to pay that loan off, he'd come in really dressed up, and he would take the banker down the street to the Stetson store and buy a new hat for the banker and for himself.

The Potato Master

Dad got quite sophisticated about growing plants, and taught me what he knew. For example, finding enough water for the crops was tricky business throughout most of the early 1930s. So Dad installed a little, 4-inch well with an electronic motor on the highest point on our 3 and ¾ acres. From there, the water ran right down the ditches we dug to irrigate our plants. Even when it was really dry, this way we could produce at least a little moisture. Not until 1937 did we get good rains throughout West Texas.

The best thing that well water ever did was help us grow potatoes, which proved to be one of our most successful crops. We excelled at growing potatoes because Dad had a special method for cultivating them. He always strived to get a smooth, round potato to market, with no ridges, and he found the perfect way to do it. Much of his land was sandy, so that helped—the soil didn't put much pressure on the plants. So we already had an edge when it came to growing potatoes.

But there was much more to it. According to his own design, Dad would plant the potatoes in 33-inch, raised rows, again making sure that there wasn't much pressure on them as they grew. So when we harvested, they came out smooth and nicely proportioned, almost every one.

Later we bought 160 acres, and Dad gave me forty of them, the choicest part of the new land. At the time he said, "It's going to be a dry year, so we ought to borrow money to put in a well here to make a giant field of sweet potatoes. If we do that, we can pay for the well in one year."

And that's exactly what happened: Dad borrowed $3400 to put in that well, and that year we made exactly $3400 selling sweet potatoes from that field. Dad had a knack for that kind of a thing.

We planted most of the rest of the land with squash, and man were we busy. Sometimes, we'd have 25 workers in the fields. When it came time to harvest, I was in charge of that, year after year. I didn't stop for breakfast, lunch or supper.

In the mornings, I'd just take three potatoes, put them in my pocket, and at noon I'd eat those potatoes and keep going. I'd just eat what we had in the garden, cucumbers and tomatoes, and keep going, because time was of the essence, to get the job done.

We also used a kiln to excel in the potato business. Dad built it a simple way—he had a way of doing things to save money. There was a Spanish fellow in town who ran the stores, and he picked up the tomato and grape lugs and the orange crates, and we'd buy them by the thousands from him. Then Dad went to see the lumberyard man and made a deal to get some white pine that was a foot wide.

We used it all to make boxes, fill them with dirt for the walls of our kiln, and then nailed tarpaper on it to make it waterproof. Then we put wire and stucco on the inside and out. When it was all done, he put six little holes in the front, and put a gas line to that. When we filled it up and closed it in the fall, we'd turn the gas heat on and heat it to 80 degrees, until the potatoes were about to sprout. Then he ventilated it until he got it down to 36 degrees, and shut it up for the winter.

The potatoes would come out cured. They were a perfect shape, and just the right size, and when people would bake one of those potatoes, syrup would run out the ends. Man, you talk about delicious! We were able to sell them for $3.50 a bushel when a bushel of regular field potatoes was selling for just $1.50.

I was with Dad when he went to a big food market that covered two city blocks. The man who ran it said, "Well, I don't need any potatoes—I just bought 43 bushels." Dad said, "Just let me bring in one bushel of ours. I'll give it to you. I'll set it on the floor, and you can sell it for whatever you want to sell it for, and you let me know after that what your judgment is."

Soon after that he called Dad, and put the other potatoes in the garbage and replaced them all with Dad's potatoes, and sold them for ten times the price of the others.

In fact, the state Agriculture Department came in to see what we were doing, and made a pamphlet about the method that they sent out to other farmers. We had discovered a method that others wanted to follow.

A Turnip Crop

One year, Dad said, "Let's grow turnips." I had some acreage next to the family land, which I usually sowed in wheat for my cows. But this year, we sowed a big plot with turnips. We had big rains that fall, and produced a super crop of huge turnips. They were some of the biggest I've seen, several inches across, and they were the perfect tenderness for eating.

But the word came one day that we were in for a hard frost, so Dad and I decided to harvest them. We pulled them all up and put them in an 8 by 12-foot hole to store them for a while. We covered them up just right so they could cure for a bit in the ground, and ate a good many of them ourselves though the winter.

Now in our small town, there were only a couple of good grocery stores, and they didn't always have access to the best produce. So, come January, we started to sell those sweet turnips for $3.50 a bushel. We couldn't begin to satisfy the market, because they were so delicious and demand for them was so high.

Some of my favorite work:
tending to the plants in a greenhouse.

The Biggest Harvest

Years later, in 1944, I went back to Lubbock to help my dad with a harvest. The year before, he'd asked me to get him two bushels of a special kind of sweet potato variety, the "Maryland Sweet." I sent the potatoes to him, and promised him that if he would do a big sweet potato planting that year, I would come down and help him harvest them.

I took my new wife, Margaret, with me. We stayed there in a two-room house my Dad provided. It didn't have any bathroom, but we had a nice outhouse. I worked sunup to sundown in the potato fields, and meanwhile, she worked at home, canning food for us. She canned 1,200 pints of food so we'd have a good amount to start our new life with, like all newlyweds should have.

Since we had a lot of tomatoes and hot peppers, I talked Margaret into making some ketchup. Now, she'd never had much contact with real hot peppers before, and ours were quite hot. So one day, she was testing the peppers to see how hot they were, and touched one to her tongue. Well, it burned her so bad that she had to quit working for the day and drink about six gallons of water. That ketchup project almost cost me a divorce!

But the sweet potato harvest went splendidly; it proved to be my Dad's biggest ever. By the time we were done, we had gathered 25,000 bushels!

This was a big deal for us and for anyone around us who was paying attention. Still, I was surprised at what happened on the last day of the harvest. As I worked on the last couple of rows, a limousine pulled up on the curb of the nearby highway, and two distinguished gentlemen dressed in black suits got out and came walking over to me where I was sitting on the tractor.

I met them on the ground, and I took off my right glove to shake their hands. They told me they were from the food industry and the U.S. Agriculture Department. Together they were working on a major new initiative to produce potato chips from sweet potatoes.

"We need you, your country needs you," they said. They seemed to know all about me, which scared the devil out of me. "We're ready to make you an offer of $25,000 a year salary with the US government," they said, and my ears did perk up, because that was a lot of money at the time. They wanted me to plant 5,000 acres of potatoes that year, 10,000 the next year, and so on. They had dehydration and slicing plants set up to make potato chips to feed folks at home and to support the war effort. "As long as the war is going on," they said, "we'd like to have you."

I respectfully declined, telling them that while I was honored by their offer, I had just signed a contract to go to North Carolina to be in the ministry. "And I must go," I said.

Looking back on it all, those early years cultivating the earth taught me one thing in particular: That it was a privilege to grow up with a Dad who grew up on a farm and had some bright ideas and determination, so we could do this type of work during the hard days of the Depression. That's how we bounced back, and then that's how we got ahead. Dad just had that ability. I don't know where he got it from, but he had it. He may have only had a third grade education, but I wish I knew today what he knew then.

CHAPTER FOUR

College Days

Working the Mill

After completing my elementary education, I went to school 330 miles away from home, in Keene, Texas, near Fort Worth. I was there from the ninth grade through my sophomore year in junior college. My sisters went to school there as well. That was quite an ordeal, to be so far away from home, and we worked our way through.

I took a job at the college mill, where they manufactured step ladders, wooden toys and so on. They put me on two tasks: Running a saw blade and running an electric sander. I worked many nights from 7:00 p.m. until 3:00 in the morning. I worked fast, and I was able to make considerably more than hour time doing piece work. That paid the bills for me.

Then I had to decide where to finish college. And since I was working my way, the whole way, I wanted to go to a college that had a mill. So I applied to Washington Missionary College in Takoma Park, Maryland, and they accepted me in 1942 and gave me a job in their mill.

I was there when they started using a new hydraulic boring machine in their mill—or at least tried to use it. They had 14 different students try out on the machine, but none of them had caught on. So the foreman of the shop, a Mr. Hotenstein, who had been impressed with my industry on other machines, said, "We've had this problem, because no one can successfully run this machine, and we really need it for our operations. Would you be interested?"

I said that of course I would, and that I could handle it. Hotenstein said, "Well, good then, we'll give you 30 days to make your jigs," (by which he meant patterns). "Then, we'll pay you for piece work after that, for as long as you work at the mill." Well that was a promise I would hold his feet to the fire on.

I backed off, and gave serious study as to how to proceed. I decided to do three things: First, I asked my roommate to go to his foreman and get me 3,000 carbon forms, in triplicate, so that I could document everything I did. I would put one copy on the finished work, one on my time card, and one for my own records. That way there would be no dispute about just how much work I had completed.

After the 30 days, I set to work with my jigs. I set everything up just right so that I could bore nine holes at a time, and I worked that machine like a Ford V-8 piston! I mastered the situation, and on their piece work rate, so it proved very profitable.

Before long, I could count on a terrific income. Even on the student's annual picnic day, I spent the morning in the mill and cranked out $87 dollars worth of piece work. I had it pretty good, for a student working in a mill.

Well, the day came when Mr. Hotenstein came to me and said, "Melvin, they're looking at your records. Everything you've produced is documented, and they couldn't find anything wrong—except you're making too much money." I was working so fast that I was making even more money than the college paid its president, and this got some administrators hot under the collar.

I replied, "Well, now, you remember that when you came to me and said you had others that couldn't do it, even at 17 cents an hour, and turned this over to me, I mastered it. And I was very meticulous with my counts, and always had the foreman check the quality of all my work. And we had an agreement that you'd pay me for piece work, as long as I worked here."

Then he brought Mr. Hoover, the mill manager, into the conversation. I gave them both a little speech: "Gentleman, I'm working with you both in a Christian institution, and I believe in fair and correct practice. The fact that no one else could do this sets my work apart. Now then, if there's fault with what I've done, I stand to be corrected. But short of that, I went to work for you under this piece work agreement. I also made a commitment not to work anywhere else while I work for you. But I came up here to get an education, not necessarily to work. I have found that I make much better grades when I'm working part time instead of loafing, and besides, I enjoy my work. I intend to work for the college and no where else until our contract is through. But I've got the money in the bank to finish my education, so I can stop working if that's what you want."

Well, then, they said, you just keep on doing what you're doing. So then, Hotenstein and Hoover went to the college business manager with all this, but he said, "Sorry, Melvin's just making too much money." They'd pay me my rate for the rest of the year, but no longer.

Funny thing happened though. At the end of the year, Hotenstein joined the service and Hoover left the college, leaving the administration with a big need for someone to run the mill. And so they ate humble pie—they came to me and asked me to do it. But I didn't want to, since I was just 22 and didn't want all that responsibility. Furthermore, the Carolina Conference of Seventh-Day Adventists had already signed me up to sell religious books in the summer, so it was just about time for me to move on from the mill work.

A Summer Selling Books

In the summer of 1943, I went to North Carolina and landed at Ballard's Crossroads, near Greenville. I was working for the Carolina Conference, supervising 25 students doing sales work. I was paid $4 a day, monitoring book sales all over Eastern North Carolina, from the coast to Raleigh. I stayed with a family, the Tysons, which kept a number of students in their house during the summer.

The first night I was there, the house was so packed they put me and two other fellows in double bed. We were tired and we slept fine, but we sure did get up quick in the morning. The windows of our bedroom were open, and one of the Tysons' mules stuck his head in and snatched the sheet right off of us! He took it out the in the yard and shook it around, and it was clear we weren't getting it back after that. And then, the flies tore into us—they came in through the window too, and without that sheet to cover us, the flies had open season on us three.

I went on the road to sell books and
pay my way through school.

From then on, we had great times together, a lifetime of friendship. They were a wonderful family. And they helped me help other folks. On a good day, I'd help these students, some of them, make $187 a day.

Doing this colporteur work, we had a nice fellow who supervised our sales, Mr. J.A.P. Green. He and I got along well, and one week he went on a sales run with me. We went from house to house, and at one big farm house they offered to let us eat dinner and stay with them for the night. They had a huge spread for us, everything two hungry salesmen could want.

Later they put us up for the night and had us share a bed. But when I woke up in the middle of the night, I noticed Mr. Green wasn't in the bed. I peered across the room and there he was, snoozing all curled up in a chair. "Mr. Green," I said, "what are you sleeping over there for?"

"I had to move, Melvin," he said. "You kicked me out of bed seven times!"

Well, that was bad enough, but then he went back to my college the next year and told everyone about how I kicked him out of bed. Oh no, I thought, now how am I ever going to find a wife with stories like these floating around?

When summer was finished, I had two weeks to spare before I went back to college. So I spent a week in the territory around Conway, South Carolina, where I went out on foot with my prospectus that demonstrated the Bible readings I was selling for $4.75 a volume.

It was wartime, and there were shortages of things to read, so people were glad to see me and to buy the books. For example, one day I was just sitting on a porch in a house where I was staying, and a man pulled up in a horse and buggy and called me over. He bought seven books right off the bat.

Things continued to go well, though I was working with meager resources. I'd hitchhike, and spend the night with a customer who was a Sunday school teacher. It was my promised obligation to call on every section in my area, no matter how remote. During the first few days, I had covered almost all the area, except for the end of a dirt road. A businessman lived there, and when I finally got to see him, he bought $147 worth of Bible story books!

That was the end of a very good week of selling books. Throughout all of my time working, I have never met such a fine group of people as I met then and there. Every one of them made me feel welcome. And by the time I reached the end of that dirt road, I had earned full scholarships—board, tuition and everything—for my sister and I.

Ambulance Driving

That fall I began my senior year at Washington Missionary College, and it was to be an exciting year. I worked as the assistant dean of men, and the job left me with some spare time for other work. My buddy, Herman "Tex" Davis, was working as an ambulance driver for a funeral home, and he asked me to come ride along, because he needed someone to carry the other side of the stretchers and caskets that he would transport. He told me that I'd make between $20 and $40 dollars per trip. I said, "Let's go."

Not only was it good money, but man was it fun. We'd go at any time of the day or night, as we were needed. We'd turn that siren on and fly through the streets of Washington. Let me tell you, roaring down Pennsylvania Avenue at two in the morning with the siren open wide was quite an experience.

Of course, sometimes the work was somewhat grisly, like the time we had to carry bodies back from a terrible train wreck on the edge of Washington. Through it all, Herman and I forged a great friendship, a lifetime friendship (today he lives near us in Fletcher, North

Carolina), and it gave me an education of how to be of help in emergencies.

"The Eyes of Texas"

The assistant dean job also gave me the chance to meet many interesting and prestigious people, like a student named Margaret Davis who would later become my wife.

I had a neat trick to get to know Margaret better. Since I had a respected job as an assistant men's dean, sometimes faculty members would have me baby-sit their kids. There was one cute little girl, in particular, that I would take care of, Elder Carrier's daughter. She was an adorable kid, with curly golden locks. Later in life she became an ice skating champion.

Well, I figured that Margaret would have a soft spot in her heart for little girls, so I always made sure we played somewhere close to where we would encounter Margaret. And sure enough, that baby-sitting stint proved to be a great way to get some attention from Margaret.

It was funny, once she and I started courting, a lot of people paid attention. She used to get ribbed about it, walking across campus, as my buddies would sing, "The eyes of Texas are upon you . . . ."

Courting

Now in our college days, we accomplished some of the purposes that we set out to accomplish there. One of them, of course, was education—to put a degree under my belt. But there were some sidelines too. Like my girlfriend, for instance.

Margaret Davis on the Chesapeake Bay in the spring of 1944, about the time I flipped for her.

Margaret was president of the Halcyon Club, the women's student organization, while I was president of the men's club. We caught on to each other fast. As president of the girl's club, it was her responsibility to look after decorations for the annual events like the fall festival. So, with an event coming up, she'd call the boy's dormitory for some help—fully realizing that I'd be the one who'd be answering the phone. She'd ask me to grab a couple guys and join her and her friends to go pick up some greenery to decorate with.

One of those days it was raining, but we went anyway. Later I found out that she went all through her dormitory to borrow the smallest umbrella she could find. And, of course, what's a gentleman to do, except carry a gal's umbrella for her and share the space with her—no matter how small the space. We weren't together yet, but we sure caught on quick.

Back in those days, though, the college was very strict about contact between the men and women. We weren't supposed to be alone without a chaperone. One night, we decided to slip away in my car and sit up on the mountain. There was supposed to be a program on campus that night, so we expected no one would miss us. But lo and behold, when we drove back, the campus was crawling with people because the program had been canceled! So I let Margaret out near the gate and made my way off in the car; fortunately no one saw us, and we never heard a word about it. We had some lucky breaks.

During spring break in our senior year, we got permission to take a trip with a chaperone to Norfolk, where Margaret had some family. The chaperone was only temporary, however, because as soon as we'd driven with him to the closest bus stop, he got out and took the bus home. So we were on our own from there on out, and again we got away with it.

Margaret and I got married the day after we graduated, June 12, 1944, in the Takoma Park Church. She was 21 and I was 24—old enough to know better, but we did it anyway!

The Diplomat's Car

One day, between classes, I was working in the den of the men's dormitory. A friend of mine gave me a call and told me to have a look at the car ads in the newspaper. I looked and saw exactly what he was talking about: A fellow was selling a like-new 1942 Mercury Coup—just what a college boy needed. The ad said: "Come to the Turkish Embassy in Washington, I'm being transferred out of the country and need to make this sale soon."

These were special circumstances, so I had to jump on it. The law at the time, because of rationing for the war effort, said that you couldn't buy a new car without a priority permit. So I called him right then, and he told me that he'd had six calls already—and that he'd told everyone, first come, first serve. I was 12 miles away, so I jumped in a car with a buddy and flew down there.

Amazingly, we were the first ones there. The Turkish diplomat came out. "I meant what I said," he told me. "You were the seventh person to call, but the first to show up, so the car's yours if you want it."

We got in the Mercury, and he let me take it for a test drive around the block. It drove beautifully. When we came back, there was a big Cadillac sitting on the curb, with a used car salesmen sitting in it. He wanted that car bad, and thought he'd get it, but he hadn't counted on us showing up first. I didn't waste any time. I said, "I'll take it."

Then the car salesman tried to outbid me, offering more money for the car. But the Turk wasn't having it. "I said first come, first serve," he said. "Who do you think I am? I cannot be bought. I said what I meant and I'm sticking to it."

I bought the car on the spot, and bought a nice camera from the fellow to boot. That was a close call, but I got the car I wanted. Before long, Margaret and I were driving it to Niagara Falls in Canada for our honeymoon.

Picturing Success

All through college, I had wonderful teachers. But my last semester, I was as busy as I'd ever been with work, and I was courting Margaret, so to be honest I didn't have much time to crack the books.

College was as fun as it was busy.

Now, I'll tell you the truth about how I got through that semester: I kept that camera around my neck. I always had it on, just in case there was something I wanted to take a picture of. One day, my Western History professor asked me to stay after class. I was worried and thought, "What have I done?"

But it wasn't bad at all. He said, "I notice you have a camera with you, and that you like to take pictures. Now, I recently built three two-story apartment buildings near campus that I want to rent out. Would you be so kind as to go and take some pictures of them for me?"

Well, I knew what to do. I took two rolls of film on those apartments, and had them developed, in color. I picked out the three best photos, had them enlarged and then framed them in gold-painted triple frame. It was more than the professor could have hoped for; when I gave them to him after one class, he was *so* appreciative. He thanked me over and over and over.

So about three weeks later it came time for our final exam in European History. He told us to put our books under our desks and take out some paper. "We'll have an oral exam, just one question. And how you answer that question will determine your entire grade for the semester."

He came to me and said. "Charlemagne. Tell me about Charlemagne, what he did, and why it was important." Well, I didn't know what to write—I didn't know Charlemagne, wasn't acquainted with him at all. I'd been too busy courting all semester to know things like that!

Still, I had to write something. So here's what I wrote: "Charlemagne, that great, great European general. He marched on the faced of the earth, bringing fear and trembling to people everywhere. Conquering and to conquer, Charlemagne." I'm telling you the actual facts, that's what I wrote.

My professor had a look. After a bit, he said, "Well, here's what you meant to say"—and he proceeded to answer the question. And not only did he give me an A in that class, I also got A's in my two other history classes that same professor taught! Now, I may not have learned much about Charlemagne, but I sure learned enough of *something* to get me through college.

CHAPTER FIVE

Church Building

Where were you?

In the winter of 1944, I started doing fulltime work for the Seventh-Day Adventist church. My first assignment was in Nashville, Tennessee, where I was to help run a series of large evangelical meetings. When I arrived there, I was wearing dungarees and pulling a trailer behind my truck. We were greeted by the maid of the evangelist I'd be working with, and she said: "They've sent you a farmer from Texas!"

Of course that didn't bother me any, and I went right to work helping with the meetings. Before long, he put me to work doing all his announcing. Sometimes we had as many as 5,000 guests at our meetings, and I enjoyed it immensely. I fancied myself to be a rather eloquent speaker—except for this one time. We had a college choir group visiting, and as I introduced them, I said, "Now, the Collegedale choir will render that beautiful hymn, 'Where Were You?'" But I'd said the wrong title—the song was actually titled, "Were You There?"

When the curtain came up, many in choir were snickering at my mistake, and some of them had trouble getting on key, they were so cracked up. They pulled it together, but from then on, whenever I'd run into one of those folks, they'd crack a smile and say to me, "Where were you?"

Free Furniture

A few months later, when those meetings ended, I was assigned by the Carolina Conference to a pastorate in Winston-Salem and Highpoint, North Carolina.

When we transferred, Margaret was pregnant with our first child, so we decided we'd need a house. Before that, we'd just been staying in apartments, and that just wouldn't do anymore. I took leave from work to build the house, and meanwhile, Margaret went out canvassing, selling books so we'd be sure to have grocery money.

So I searched around a bit and found a lot I liked and bought it for $408. I hired a talented local brick mason, a Mr. Messick, to help me get a house off the ground. He was so respected that the lumber company was happy to finance the house construction for us. I also hired a carpenter, a Mr. Moore, at $1.25 an hour. He was quite a worker. When we started building, he sat me down and said, "I'm going to tell you how I work. While I'm working, I won't be stopping to talk to you or anything else. I'll talk to you at lunch or after work. It's your time, and while I'm on it, I'm going to be working every moment for your benefit." He was certainly a fine gentleman. He stayed with me through thick and thin, until we'd completed a six-room house with a basement.

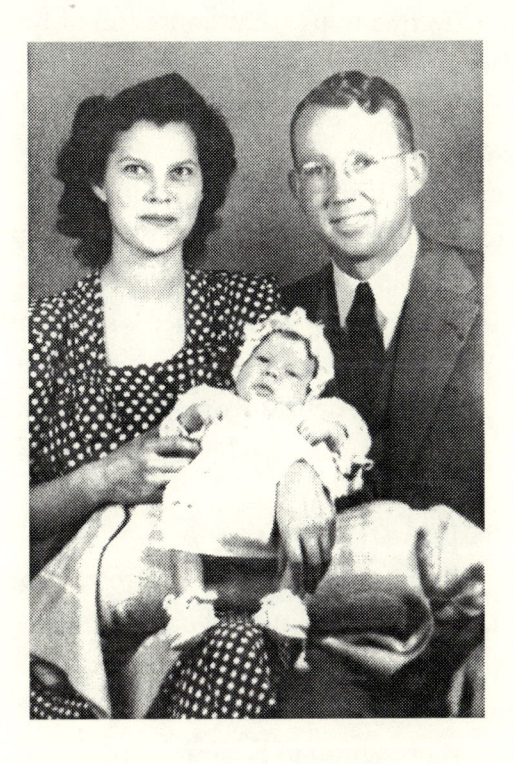

Margaret and I with our firstborn,
Bruce, in Winston-Salem in 1946.

It was a sturdy house, but an empty one, since we didn't have so much as a stick or furniture. The very day we finished building it, after I put on the last coat of paint, I picked up a newspaper and began reading it. One want-ad jumped out at me: A man was seeking an apartment to rent and a place to store a house full of furniture. I called the man and told him where we were. He said, "I'll take it, and I'll be there in five minutes."

We got along splendidly, and had set up a sweet deal before we knew each other for half an hour. And then he told us we were free to use that house full of furniture for free—tables, lamps, bedroom suites, a refrigerator, the whole ball of wax—until we got on our feet and could afford to buy our own.

We rented the three upstairs rooms to him for $60 a month. But that very day I met him, when he sat down an wrote us a check, he said: "I know that you're under some strain, having just built this house, here's six months rent in advance." Well that got us started in great shape, a young, married couple, free of debt and owning our own, furnished house. We lived there comfortably and felt really blessed.

The "Chapel of Faith"

I was in Winston-Salem for almost two years before I was transferred, and this move turned out to be one of the best things that ever happened to me.

The president of the conference said, "We have a large area for you to cover, most of Eastern North Carolina. There are seven 'companies' of believers out there now, but there's not one church building. We want you to go out there and build some churches."

I was 25 at the time, and it would be a tremendous challenge. We lived in Kinston, in the middle of our new district. These seven groups were meeting in all sorts of places, in houses, school rooms and print shops, whatever spaces we could get access to. I impressed upon them all that they needed church buildings, but most of them wouldn't go for it at first, because it seemed like such a big undertaking. They needed to see it done correctly first, they needed an example.

That example sprang up in the town of Newbern. There were two believers there who were ready to make a big move. One was a fellow, Mr. C. Foy Keen, who was crippled a bit and used a wheelchair, but he was intent on building a church. He said, "Brother Elliston, if you'll drive the nails, I'll do the soliciting." So that's how we handled it.

The other believer was a widow woman, a Ms. Bailey, who worked in a mill and had six children. She wanted to help out, but of course her means were very limited. Lately she'd only had occasional work, as the mill would call her in once every few days. I asked her, "Sister Bailey, which day do they call you in the least on?" She said that day was Monday, that she almost never got called in on a Monday. Well, I didn't want to burden her much, so I suggested, "If you like, you can share your Monday wages, if you come to have any, with the church effort." She agreed to do that, but was skeptical, since she hardly ever worked that day.

But wouldn't you know, the very next Monday she was called in to the mill, and the 10 Mondays after that!

By then, we'd just about finished building the new church. On the twelfth Monday, Ms. Bailey wasn't called in to the mill, so instead she came to the church and washed the windows for us, so they'd be clean for our first service. Her case made me think of the Bible story of the widow with only two mites. She gave them both—all the money she had—to the temple in Jerusalem. And Jesus, observing this, called his disciples together and told them: "Verily I say unto you, that this poor widow hath cast more in than all they which have cast into the treasury."

It had taken a great deal of work and good fortune to get that church off the ground. When I got to the site we'd chosen, the concrete slab was poured, but that was it. The grass, vines and weeds were ten feet high around that slab, so I decided to tackle that first. One August day, I set to cutting it all down, to get some air circulating, but man was it hot. Before long I was sweating like crazy, and worse, I'd forgotten to bring along my ice-water bottle along with me that day. I got hot and bothered real fast.

I had another problem to think about that day. There was a man and woman who had a home next to our church lot, and they had already made it clear that they were not happy with us building next door, and that they were going to raise a stink about it. Still, I needed some water something fierce, so I decided to go see them and ask for a drink.

Well, the man wasn't home, but the woman saw me coming, and came storming out to meet me; it was clear she was about to let me have it, about to tell me exactly what she thought of her new neighbors. But before she could get a word out, I wiped my sweaty brow and said, quietly, "Lady, can you spare a glass of cold water?"

She was totally disarmed. "Why, of course," she said, inviting me up to her porch. She brought me cup after cup of cold water, until I'd had about seven. I took my time drinking them, getting to know her a bit. And, lo and behold, sharing the water seemed to melt away all her anger about our church—it did her just as much good as it did me. She was nothing but friendly, and didn't say anything against us building next door.

Three days later, she and her husband walked over to the lot and invited me to dinner that evening. We struck up a friendship, and I ate with them many, many times thereafter. They even came to our church's dedication, and they never spoke against it again. And then, finally, after we had completed the church and just before I was transferred, she said, "Mr. Elliston, do you have any idea what I was going to say to you that day you asked me for water?" I said, "Yes ma'am, but I'm sure glad you changed your mind." She said that when I asked her for that cold water, her anger and suspicions about the church just melted.

Meanwhile, I'd been spreading the word to all of the other companies, letting them know that we were getting a church off the ground in Newbern. I invited them all to join us for our first service, and about 150 of them came. The pews were full and people were standing in the isles. It was a great day, and V.G. Anderson, president of the Southern Union of Seventh-Day Adventists, came up from Atlanta to give the dedicatory sermon.

And that wasn't all. The whole time we'd been raising funds and building the church, I'd been giving bible studies in the local area, and picked up some new recruits. The day of our first service, we baptized 12 new members into what had started as a two-member church. My wife, Margaret, decided to call the Newbern church the "Chapel of Faith," because just a few people's faith had gotten it off the ground.

Spreading the Word

Now the seeds were planted. Our success in Newbern—in just 12 weeks—set the pace for the other groups of believers that we were reaching out to. To see those two enterprising people get the ball rolling on their own in Newbern just electrified all the other groups. People with money in the other companies started standing in line to ask me when I was going to build them a church too. We were swamped from then on.

Here I am as a young evangelist,
along with a colleague and his son.

Next, we decided to build a church in Goldsboro, and pledged to have it up and running within 40 days and 40 nights. And we did it! There we were assisted by one of the finest gentlemen I ever knew, Mr. L.K. Stallings, who helped run a large hardware store. He was an extremely dignified and honorable man, and with him leading the local company of believers, our time in Goldsboro was always a joy.

Then we set to building one church after another, in Greenville, Rocky Mount, Wilson, Plymouth, Elizabeth City, Asheboro, Kernersville, Roanoke Rapids, Wilmington and other towns. During my five years in the district, I had the privilege to help build a total of 17 new churches. As fast as we could build the churches, the conference backed us up, sending new pastors to handle the new congregations while I moved on to the next project.

During that time we were church-building, the Southern

Union sent a man to accompany me on visits to folks who had taken the church's Bible study correspondence course. We'd go all day, checking in on people who had filled out a card expressing their interest in learning more.

On one of these trips, we set out real early in the morning, and I said to my partner, somewhat facetiously, that I'm going to stop at the next house and see if they'll fix us breakfast. What he didn't know, and I did, was that the woman living there, a Mrs. Langley, was already a member of the church, and that I was getting mighty close to getting her husband to enter the faith as well.

So I parked the car and said, "Hold on, I'll be right back after I ask them for a free breakfast." He must have thought I was crazy, because I knocked on the door and they opened it, still wearing their pajamas. Well, they invited us in and said "Sure, we'll fix you breakfast." Mr. Langley built a wood fire in the stove, and his wife started making biscuits. They were great hosts, we had a great time together, and it provided me with a chance to nudge the man a bit toward making a decision.

I could tell he was showing signs of greater interest in the church, and his wife thought so too. So a couple of weeks later, when they invited us over for a Saturday lunch, I decided to see if he'd commit. After the meal, he and I went for a walk down to the Neuse River. I had never called him "Brother" before, always "Mr." But I felt like warming things up now, so this day, I began "Brother Langley."

"Brother Langley," I said, "we're dedicating a new church, and I've put in a baptistery underneath the rostrum, because I anticipate the need to baptize people like you. Will you join us?"

And he said, "Yes, I will," just like that.

There were some bittersweet times too. Just before I was to transfer out again, I had a lunch with Mr. L.K. Stylings, a wonderful, polished gentleman who worked in the hardware business and had been a great help to us in the church efforts. He said to me, "Brother Elliston, it has been wonderful to have you here and to found this new church. Now, you're leaving soon, so I probably won't see you again in this life, but I'll see you on the other side." And two weeks later, he passed on. We missed him greatly, but I knew he was right, that we'd see him again one day.

And of course, it was never easy, getting a new church built, no matter how much help and good will we had supporting us. In Rocky Mount, for example, we'd built the frame for the building when, one night, a terrible windstorm came through town. I knew we had to keep those frames up, so I went out there at three in the morning to build some braces. It was raining, the wind was blowing hard, and the hail was about to start falling. But I did what I had to do to make the project go forward, and I didn't mind doing it.

Kernersville

In Kernersville we built what was, at the time, that town's biggest church. We built the membership with a series of popular meetings called, "My Mother's old Bible is True, from Cover to Cover Through." A wonderful singer, Wally Fowler, provided just the right music for us. By the time we were done, we had 37 new members, which meant that we led the Carolina Conference in baptisms that year.

We had some interesting experiences there, to say the least. One day, after I'd done some painting at our new church, I was driving out and accidentally hit the back of another car that was passing in front of the church. I got out and shook hands with the man and gave him my information. I said, "I'd be glad to call the highway patrol," but he said, "Don't worry about it, we can handle it."

Even considering the circumstances, we got along great. Believe it or not, a few weeks later, I baptized him, his wife and their two children into our new Kernersville church! The good book says to go out on the highways and hedges and bring 'em in, and I guess that's exactly what I did that day.

When we were dedicating the church, I made an alter call, and everyone but three individuals came forward. You know, all preachers are just a little bit facetious sometimes, and, with every head bowed, I had a little peek to see who was out there. I'm not exactly sure why I did it, but then, I said in reverent tones, "Would to God that all had of come forward today." Of course, then, everyone else had to peak and see who didn't come forward. Well, that cured my problem with at least one of them: One of the three, a woman, came forward, and said she realized she'd been on the wrong side of the fence and wanted to join us in prayer.

Greenville and Wilmington

In Greenville, I found many life-long friends. The leader of the church group there was Jack Tyson, and he often took me raccoon hunting. One night we went out, he and his buddy had trained bloodhounds with them. They also had a bulldog, and I could tell that dog wanted to go along. They didn't think he'd be much help, but I had a hunch.

So we loaded up the dogs and headed down near the

Neuse River. It had been terribly dry that summer, and consequently the dogs had a terrible time trying to pick up scents. After a while, the trained hounds came back to us— they'd given up. But the bulldog was missing, and before you knew it, we found out he'd treed a coon! We found that dog at the base of the tree barking up a storm.

Well, it probably goes without saying, but I'll say it anyway: I had a great time kidding my friends about how my supposedly no-count bulldog had done what their purebred hounds had failed to do.

I loved working down near the coast, too. When we were church-building in Wilmington, we had a wonderful man who was a brick mason working with us. He would take me bass fishing and we'd service his eel traps. There was also a doctor in the church who had a 16-foot boat, and he would take me fishing in the ocean.

The first time we went, we stopped at a diner on the way where I stuffed myself with pancakes. That was a big mistake, I found out later. The ocean wasn't smooth that day, and the waves were pitching us about, and I got terribly seasick. It's a wonder I lived through that, I was so torn up. I guess it was one more reminder that sometimes, the Lord takes care of foolish children.

The "Lazy Preacher"

I didn't mind the hard work involved in building these churches; in fact, I was always happier when I had some work to do. I'd work six days a week, 12 hours a day or more on many of the churches, and people responded positively to that. The harder I'd work, the harder they'd work too.

Well, one day we stopped by to see some colporteurs in the town of Washington, and I was exhausted from all the work we'd been doing. So I leaned up against the wall to relax for just a moment. And right then, a little girl, someone's daughter, walked up to me and blurted out "Lazy preacher!"

Just like that, I had a new nickname. Calling me lazy was ironic, to be sure, but I always liked it.

After we'd built a church in Asheboro, it came time for me to switch gears a bit. The brethren at the Carolina Conference office in Charlotte asked me to come work with them as a promoter and fundraiser. For the next several years, I was the conference's top fundraiser. But I sure did miss being an evangelist on the go. I've regretted it ever since, accepting this responsibility as a promoter, instead of staying out on the firing line working with the churches. I could have done it for the rest of my days.

CHAPTER SIX

Taking Care of Business

The Catalina Motel

In the 1950s we relocated to the deep South, and I helped the church build a new high school, Bass Memorial Academy in Mississippi. Then, after many years of mostly doing church work, you might say I returned to my early ways of entrepreneurship. Ever since I was young, I'd felt the urge to run my own businesses and projects, so finally I succumbed to that urge.

One thing I'd always wanted to do was own a motel. When we were living in Huntsville, Alabama, during the early 1960s, I found a way to do it. A man was selling a motel there—he called it the Edge of Town Motel.

A partner and I bought it from him, but I wasn't going

to call my motel the "Edge of Town," no sir. We renamed it the Catalina Motel. It was a good-looking place. We had a huge sign, the size of those big Holiday Inn signs, and our office had a huge glass facade.

When we bought it, it had 28 units, and we added 28 more units, a new business office and a laundry room. We tried to make everything as modern as possible. By 1964, we had everything upgraded, and we were doing business.

On the same property, we ran one of the best restaurants in town, "The Stork Club." We had terrific business from all over Huntsville. For awhile, we were there at a good time. Our business was near some major research centers, and the town was growing rapidly.

The business grew and grew for about four years. Eventually we took on as many as 12 employees as we grew, between the managers, maids and landscapers and such. We also did a lot of the work ourselves, Margaret and I. Eventually we agreed to buy my partner out, so we owned the whole thing.

There were some adventures. We were robbed several times, but fortunately nobody got hurt.

Over time, our business began to ebb a bit. Huntsville got many bigger motels, so we had lots of competition. There were good years and bad years, but the competition was starting to really chip away at our business when we were touched by luck: The state highway department decided they wanted to place a new freeway straight through our property.

When the department did a thorough appraisal of the property, then we negotiated a bit and wound up cashing out for a very comfortable figure. By then we'd had the motel for 20 years.

On the day we closed, I asked my banker to go down to

the lawyer's office with me to pick up the check. He was a good friend, but he said, "Now, I don't really need to go down there with you."

But I said, "You've been so longsuffering and such a help to me, with my various endeavors, and I'd just be honored to have my bank president come down with me to get this $1 million check."

He said OK, and we walked down to the lawyer's office. Then I decided to crack a little joke with my banker. As soon as I had that check in my hands, I turned it over and endorsed it. Then I handed it to the banker and said, "Now, that check's officially deposited in the bank. So if we get held up on the way back to the bank, it's already in the bank's possession, and it's not my loss."

We got a good laugh out of that, and we got back to the bank with no trouble.

The state was going to wreck the buildings, of course, so the furniture was ours to sell and donate to charity. So we didn't do too badly at all.

Overall, that motel was a worthwhile investment for us. I've always said this: Every man needs one motel, and every man needs one restaurant. You can't make all the deals you come across, but I was glad that I had both.

The Carwash

I was a general contractor for 25 years, and the whole time my insurer was Jerry Holcomb. We were good friends even before I hired him, and he took good care of me with insurance for all of my business, property and medical matters. We remain close buddies to this day.

One day in the mid-1960s he came to my office and

said, "Put your hand on this. I want you to bless it." Then he handed me an agreement from some partners to transfer a carwash to our possession. It was a unique deal: Not only were they offering to give us the carwash, they were offering to give us $6,000 cash to take over for the lease for them.

Well you gotta sit up and look at an offer like that—but maybe we didn't look at it long enough. We'd both been talking about getting a carwash anyway, so we decided to use this opportunity to jump into the business.

The carwash was in a great location in West Huntsville, on a traffic island next to a main thoroughfare where there was lots of traffic. But we didn't know anything about the electronics you need to keep an automatic carwash running. We did have a fellow we hired to do that for us. However, we soon discovered that it cost more to keep those electronics going than it did to keep the rest of the carwash going.

But we did alright with it, and kept trying, at least. One day, we got some unexpected help when my son Roger decided that we didn't have enough business. He walked over to a competing carwash and started telling the customers, "Now, there's a better carwash around the corner. You should go over there." I put a stop to that when I heard what Roger was doing, but I sure thought it was a funny form of free advertising.

Months went by, and eventually we'd spent all of that $6,000 on keeping the electronics running and meeting the lease payments. So Jerry came up with the idea of building a second lane going through the carwash. We built it ourselves, but try as we would, we still couldn't get those electronics functioning smoothly enough to make the place profitable.

By and by, after a few more months, we decided to throw

in the towel on this project and try to market the property to someone else. We were sitting in a restaurant one day when Jerry said, "There's a fellow I know who's sitting over there, having his lunch. I'm going over there to sell him our carwash." And he went over and did just that.

Jerry convinced the fellow to buy the carwash for $12,000. By 9:15 the next morning the deal was done and the check was in the bank.

Ever since, I've said this: That was the first time I ever made money losing money.

The Shopping Center and Apartments

One of my biggest jobs while working as a general contractor was to refurbish and expand a shopping center that had fallen into pretty rough shape. The center still hosted a Winn Dixie, a U.S. Postal Office and a Gulf Oil, but that was all, and there was plenty of empty land around the property for more concerns to move in.

Over time, my various partners in the deal came to me, one by one, and said they wanted to sell their shares in the project. One by one, I made deals with them, and eventually I was the sole owner of the whole shebang.

I knew it could be a big liability, but I pressed on with it for the long hall. There was plenty of cause for discouragement along the way, but I've never been one to get discouraged.

Eventually, we improved the shopping center property significantly and its value went up considerably. And soon we had buyers, big companies, coming to us to inquire about the various lots. By the time we liquidated it, bit by bit to various buyers, we came out smelling like a rose.

When we moved to Huntsville, I decided to do other real estate projects as well. In one of the major ones, we found some acreage near the center of town, cut it up into lots and started building. Soon we were renting out 23 brick duplexes.

We gave two of those duplexes to each of our three sons, and that proved to be a fine move, one of the best we made in trying to rear and educate out kids. The money from renting those units brought in enough funds for our sons to get through college and medical school in good shape. Later, they were able to sell the units to get their own families off the ground.

My Three Sons

Of course these busy years were full of excitement with our three boys. I could write a whole book about their experiences growing up, but for now I'll tell you about some of my freshest memories of them.

The first boy, Bruce, was born in 1946. From age four, Bruce said he was going to grow up to be a doctor. When he was very young, you see, he played a doctor in a church play, and he loved it. And another time, when Margaret scratched her leg up on some thorns, he helped her dress the wounds, saying, "Mama, I doctor. I doctor Mama." And today, Bruce is a family doctor.

The second boy, Leon, was born in 1950. Now all of our children became good athletes in various sports, but Leon loved baseball most of all. He was a pitcher. In Little League, I remember, his ball cap was bigger than he was—but he played the game in a big way.

During one game Leon really showed what he was capable of. The pitcher before him had loaded the bases, and there were no outs. So the coach brought Leon in to try to resolve the situation and keep those runners from coming home. He got up on the mound and began rubbing the ball very seriously. He turned that cap around a few times, and then started pitching. What happened next was amazing: Leon pitched nine strikes in a row, getting all three of the next batters out. The crowd went wild and gave little Leon a standing ovation.

Margaret and I with our three sons,
(left to right) Roger, Bruce and Leon.

Like his brother, Leon became a doctor too: First a pediatrician and then an allergist.

Our third boy, Roger, was born in 1956. He was always a smart kid, but at one point early in the game he got the notion that he'd had enough education. When he was five, we let him ride to Texas with some friends to see his grandparents. When he got back, he declared: "I'm not going to school anymore. Papa said that he wasted three years in school, and I don't see the need of it."

I didn't say anything, I just let him go through his speech. Then I put Roger in the pickup and took him on a little ride around Huntsville. I drove him around the roughest part of town—three square blocks that were in terrible shape. As I was getting near the end of the area, he said, "What are we doing here?"

I said, "Well, I wanted to show you where you're going to live, if you don't go to school."

He made a quick decision and blurted out, "I'm going to school then!"

And Roger, too, later went into medicine. He's a dentist (and lately, he's also shown a real talent for making real estate deals).

In the 1980s, and as I'll describe in the next chapter, Margaret and I made our way back to North Carolina to live. It's been delightful to live in the Carolinas since the days of the 1940s and then to come back here as we got further on in life. We've had great fun watching our boys settle here as well, and over time their families have grown too. We've been blessed by a bunch of grandkids

Bruce and his wife Judy have three boys: Jon, who's a writer; Brian, who's finishing up a college degree in geology and will be a teacher; and Joel, who teaches physical education and is profitably working at a local grocery store. And a few years ago, a remarkable young woman named Jennifer Shelton joined their family. She just finished a degree in psychology at the University of North Carolina in Asheville.

Leon and his wife Bettie have three children: Both Andrew and Lauren are studying to become doctors, and Audrey is completing her studies at Claremont McKenna College.

CHAPTER SEVEN

(Sort of) Settling Down

Big Trips

Like I said in chapter one, I've always had a case of "goin' fever." While I've spent most of my life moving about the southern part of the United States, several times I've had the privilege to travel outside the country. The first time was in 1944, when I traveled a mere 19 miles into Canada with Margaret for our honeymoon. We went to Niagara Falls.

My next time outside the United States came when I went on a short trip to Mexico with a school group including my son, Bruce. We had a great time down there, and did some fine fishing. Bruce, knowing how fast taxi drivers could go down there, leaned up to one of our drivers and said,

"Drive fast! I want to thrill my Dad!" And let me tell you, the driver was happy to oblige.

Margaret and I during our trip to Alaska.

Then, many years later, in 1986, Margaret and I toured Brazil with a church group. What a thrill it was to visit Seventh-Day Adventist academies, churches and mission schools! We also saw some of the most beautiful waterfalls in the world, and Rio de Janeiro was a special treat.

Then, just two years ago, we traveled to Vancouver, Canada and points beyond with our son Bruce and two of his boys. This big trip included a cruise to Alaska, which was beautiful. There were plenty of wonderful things to see there, in particular the wildlife, from whales to bears to huge caribou. It was a trip long to be remembered.

But I've got to tell you the truth: The one, main reason this Texan went all the way to Alaska was to be sure—to verify the claim I've always been skeptical about—that Alaska is even bigger than Texas.

Back to Carolina

Over the years, I've moved my wife and our home 43 different times. Margaret's barely put up with it.

So the time came, around 1980, when Margaret and I decided that we wanted to find some property to settle down on for a bit, some acreage that we could improve. We weren't sure just where we'd look, but bit by bit the choice became clear.

My son Bruce and his family were living in Asheville, and he and his wife decided to take a vacation and asked Margaret and I to come stay with their kids while they were gone. We were happy to do it, and when I got to Asheville, Bruce put me in touch with a realtor who said he had some good options for us.

The realtor started by showing us 45 acres that he suggested was a good buy. The land was between two old turkey farms, and it had been cleared of all its trees. Basically, it was a bunch of stumps and a lot of yellow clay. I didn't like the looks of it, and I didn't like the smell either. But I told the fellow to call me if he had anything else of a similar size to show me.

The next day he called and said that there was a wonderful farm for sale, and that perhaps they could sell us a parcel of it. "Well, if it's somewhat desirable, I'd be happy to look at it," I said. So he took me out to this property, which totaled about 600 acres. It was off Avery's Creek Road in Arden, just south of Asheville. On one side, the property was bordered by the Blue Ridge Parkway.

Back in North Carolina with my three sons,
(left to right) Roger, Leon and Bruce.

It was lovely, but the land had been overgrazed for a few years, so I wasn't sure about the quality of it all. Still, the realtor had high hopes, and later that day he asked me if I'd be interested in the whole place. I said, "Man, what are you talking about? I'm just looking for about 40 acres." But he pushed the point, and told me that the owners would be visiting town that very night, if I wanted to talk business with them.

I said, "That's pretty far out of my league, but let's explore it." Within a day he was showing me a contract, and I realized that, if I strained a bit and pulled all my collateral together, I could work it out. I didn't waste any time. I read that contract, then pulled a pen out of my overalls and signed it. Then I had to hustle back to Huntsville, to shift some money around and make sure I could cover the check I'd put up for the down payment.

It took everything we had, but we worked it out, and came out smelling like a rose. It took us ten years to pay it all off. In the meantime, we worked it as a cattle farm, raising Polled Herefords. We got up to about 100 head when we were at our peak.

Walnut Cove

Late in their lives, my parents came up from Texas to visit us in North Carolina and have a look at our new farm, Walnut Cove. Dad and I hopped in the pickup and I toured him around the entire place. At the time, the land was in wonderful shape, and the grass in places was growing as high as the windows on the truck. "Melvin, this must be awfully rich land," he told me. I agreed. While I was still busy in Huntsville, Bruce had done plenty to get the land in great shape.

My Dad made an important point: "You've got a little Garden of Eden here. See to it that whatever you do here you add to that garden and all of its beauty."

We followed his advice. During years of hard work and total enjoyment of the place, we managed to keep a pretty good product in the form of farm agriculture. For instance, when we bought the farm it had wild thistles in several hollows on the place. So I got up with my two oldest grandboys, Brian and Jon, and I gave them a dime per plant to go out and chop the thistles down with a hoe. They found one hollow that had more than 5,000 thistles in it! I hoed plenty of them myself, as well, and over time, over the years, we got rid of those thistles.

(It reminded me of some work those boys had done for me back in Huntsville. There, we had a fine garden, and I wanted all of the bullfrogs I could get to come live in that garden and take care of the bugs for me. So when Brian and Jon would come to visit, I'd pay them a dollar a frog to collect them and bring them into the garden. Then a funny thing would happen: The frogs would hop out of the garden, heading back to their habitat, and the boys would catch them again—and collect another bounty on the same frog.)

Besides the cattle, we decided to buy a horse or two, and we ended up with twelve fine horses. We'd ride them around the farm, and take them on trail-riding trips all over Western North Carolina. Then we got some antique carts and buggies for the horses to pull. This was a great time for us. We went up to Amish settlements in Pennsylvania to get the carts. While we were up there, we bought an Amish-trained horse named Major, a pacer who used to run the races in New Jersey.

Once, in the 1980s, we put Major to use in a delightful event at the famous Biltmore Estate here in Asheville. Margaret and I put on the clothing worn by folks in the 1880s and Major pulled our buggy in a procession around the main mansion. That horse really lived it up—whenever we'd get near a crowd, he'd hold his head high and strut. There were more than 3,000 people there, and he loved them as much as they loved him. What a show it was!

Selling the Farm

Over the years, various developers showed an interest in our farm land, due to its natural beauty. And just a few years ago, we found a team of businessmen, the Cliffs organization headed by Jim Anthony, that were serious about purchasing the place. After many negotiations, we sold them 540 acres of the farm, which is now becoming the "Cliffs at Walnut Cove."

It has been a wonderful experience working with Anthony and his organization, and now they're building hundreds of first-class homes and a Jack Nicklaus golf course, which will be among the highest quality courses in the world. The beauty of it is beginning to show through, though at this writing the course is still a year or so away from being finished.

A word or two about Jim Anthony: It's a pleasure to deal with a man who, as you talk about a thing and come to an agreement, means everything he says, and does it just as he said he would do it. I've valued that fellowship and working relationship. With the reputation of the Cliffs, and Mr. Anthony in particular, it's not been hard to find buyers for the new houses, and the prospects for the whole venture look bright.

My Dog Bear

I've always loved my pets, and it's probably fair to say that I've loved Bear the most. Let me tell you about this wonderful dog.

Margaret and I had several Labrador Retrievers in our day, but a few years ago we found ourselves with no pets. Then someone contacted our son Roger and sold him a new chocolate Lab, which he named Bear. Roger kept him for a few weeks, but he realized that it was a big burden looking after the dog, and he knew we'd like to have him. He said,

"I'll give Bear to you, if you'll let him still be my dog." Well, we accepted him, with all the obligations.

Me and Bear: A better dog there never was.

We loved him from the get-go, but we went through some trials together. During one of the first walking trips Margaret took with Bear, when he was just a few weeks old, it was right after a big rain. The water had filled up our farm pond, and when it hit the overflow pipe, it was making a big splash. Well, nothing thrilled Bear like running water, and he went straight for that pipe. Then something terrible happened: When Bear got to the edge of the pipe, he managed to get himself sucked into it. It pulled him down 14 feet, and he was stuck, with water rushing over him.

We could hear him moaning, but didn't know what to do to get him out. We called the fire department, and they made a quick response, sending seven different vehicles full of men to try to help us free Bear. One of them had a powerful flashlight, so we trained that on Bear, so he'd know we were there.

Now and then, Bear would get tired and quiet down, and we wondered over and over if we had lost him. The ordeal went on for two-and-a-half hours, and we were terrified. Margaret would later say that, "You know, I had three boys, but that scare with Bear was the worst trauma I've ever gone through in my life."

We were willing to try anything. I got the tractor and tried to see if I could bust the damn and drain the lake, but I didn't get anywhere with that. Then one of the firemen had a great idea: He told me to get a length of PVC pipe, about 20 feet long, and we'd put a noose around it, push it down the pipe to snag Bear. And that's exactly what they did; they slipped the noose over Bear's nose and head, and out came the puppy!

Well, we were all relieved that Bear was saved, and right from the start, Margaret and I took to him and he took to us. He's been a perfect pet throughout his life with us.

We did have one other scare though. Sometime later, he went off chasing after a groundhog or some other creature. During the chase, poor Bear fell into a hole and did a somersault, then landed on a rock and bashed his hip. He lay there a long time, because he was really hurt. We took him to the vet and told them to do whatever it took to help him. He had developed a large blood clot, so they had to perform a major surgery to prevent him from becoming paralyzed. We spent $4,000 on fixing him up, and it was worth every penny.

I'll tell you just a bit about why Bear's so special to us. To begin with, he's a very perceptive creature, which we notice every time we take him for a walk. One time, he stopped in mid-step, with one foot in the air, and looked down to see that there was a copperhead in the grass. He looked up at me as is to say, "What do I do?" I said, "Bear, back off, don't bother that." And sure enough, he backed up nice and easy. Another time, we were walking across a grassy field, and a mama deer heard us coming and ran off in fright. Then her little fawn got up, but it was so young it could barely hobble. I said, "Now Bear, you leave that baby alone and come along with me." And he did just that. He has a great understanding of animal nature.

Bear's very attentive to us. During the entire eight years he's been with us, we've taken frequent walks in the woods. But recently, something has changed. I can tell that he's noticed his master is slowing down a bit. During our previous trips, he was always in the lead, sniffing things out and guiding us. But lately, he stays much closer to us and even lingers behind a bit, and I can tell he's looking out for us, making sure that we get out of the woods OK. He's become the watcher and keeper of his granddaddy and grandmother, and he thinks it's his place to look out for our safety, just like we've looked after his.

Some years ago, Bear decided, of his own free will, to become the "vice-president" around our house. We have two big reclining chairs in our den, and I'll sit in one while Bear sits in the other. Whenever I get out of my chair and leave the room, Bear will get up and move over to sit in my chair, with great pride. So I call him the vice-president, and he seems to like that plenty.

In the annals of people and pets, I would claim the best experience of all between me and Bear, who's sitting next to me listening to this story as I tell it.

From One Pepper Seed

Here we are in November 2003, and I want to tell the latest story of what has happened in my garden. That's right: I'm still gardening, after all these years.

In North Carolina, I've continued my life-long love of gardening. Here I am with parts of a recent harvest.

This year I planted a few stalks of different kinds of hot pepper, because I like a little spice now and then. Just the other day, I pulled up the last three stalks to harvest the peppers. One was in the center, and it was very prolific. So I got one of my wife's stew pans and counted the pods pulled from that one stalk, to see what degree of increase I'd been given from one pepper seed.

From just that one stalk there were more than 300 peppers. I'm telling the truth! On one limb alone there were 43.

Now, at this point, curiosity got the best of me. So I took two of the peppers, put on a pair of my wife's rubber gloves, so that I wouldn't get the hot pepper oil on my hands, and proceeded to count the seeds in each one of them. I cut them open, and found 65 in one and 67 in the other! Nobody may believe it, but I got a return of thousands of seeds. A lifetime supply, you might say.

Looking Back from Here

As I pause and look back through my 85 years, I feel very fortunate to be in good health and able to remember the tracks I've traveled along the way. And I haven't traveled them alone. This summer, Margaret and I celebrated 60 years together, and I've been a lucky man to have her walking side-by-side with me so long and so far.

Overall, I feel deeply blessed and deeply appreciative to have been an American from 1919 on, living through the rest of the century and on into a new one. It's been a real and continual learning experience that has taught me what it means to be an American today.

In the long history of the world, what a wonderful time to be living!

In the summer of 2004, Margaret and I celebrated our 60th wedding anniversary.

BVG